THINK BETTER
BASEBALL

THINK BETTER
BASEBALL

SECRETS FROM MAJOR LEAGUE COACHES AND PLAYERS FOR MASTERING THE MENTAL GAME

Bob Cluck

New York   Chicago   San Francisco   Lisbon   London   Madrid   Mexico City
Milan   New Delhi   San Juan   Seoul   Singapore   Sydney   Toronto

The McGraw·Hill Companies

Library of Congress Cataloging-in-Publication Data

Cluck, Bob.
  Think better baseball : secrets from major league coaches and players for mastering the mental game / Bob Cluck.
      p.   cm.
    Includes index.
    ISBN 0-8092-9714-0
    1. Baseball—United States—Psychological aspects.   2. Baseball—Coaching—United States.   I. Title.

  GV867.6 .C58   2002
  796.357'01'9—dc21   2002023613

5 6 7 8 9 10 11 12 13 14 15 16 17 18 19 20 21 22   WCT/WCT   0 9 8 7 6

ISBN-13: 978-0-8092-9714-6
ISBN-10:   0-8092-9714-0

Cover design by Nick Panos
Interior design by ABZORB Design, Inc.
Interior photographs by Teri Cluck
Thanks to model Ollie Anderson
Thanks to The Batter's Box, in Poway, California

McGraw-Hill books are available at special quantity discounts to use as premiums and sales promotions, or for use in corporate training programs. For more information, please write to the Director of Special Sales, Professional Publishing, McGraw-Hill, Two Penn Plaza, New York, NY 10121-2298. Or contact your local bookstore.

This book is printed on acid-free paper.

To Teri, Jennifer, Amber, Blanda, and Buddy

To Beatrice, Nina, and Sonny

In memory of Dennis Maley

To every kid in America who dreams of playing in the major leagues

To coaches who have sacrificed in order to make their players a little better

*To every parent who has supported the players and coaches emotionally
and helped provide the resources for youth sports to survive*

Contents

Introduction

The San Diego School of Baseball was founded in 1971. Since then, scores of the finest players, coaches, and instructors in the history of baseball have either attended or taught there. More than 10,000 students have studied at this world-famous school, which is a laboratory for learning baseball fundamentals and advanced mechanics.

Pitchers and pitching coaches have included Dave Smith, Roger Craig, Mike Scott, Don Sutton, Brent Strom, Goose Gossage, Don Alexander, Buddy Black, Dave Dravecky, Randy Jones, Bob Miller, Darryl Kile, Tom House, Kevin Hazlett, Norm Sherry, Trevor Hoffman, and others. These professionals developed concepts like the split-fingered fastball and exchanged countless ideas that have helped develop pitching instruction into an art form.

Hitters and hitting instructors like Joe Morgan, Pete Rose, Willie Stargell, Bob Skinner, Deron Johnson, Robin Yount, Tony Gwynn, Alan Trammell, Steve Garvey, George Brett, Steve Finley, Reggie Waller, Tye Waller, Jim Skaalen, Glenn Ezell, Bob Vetter, Dave Winfield, Ozzie Smith, Sparky Anderson, and others helped form what has been called a state-of-the-art philosophy concerning hitting mechanics.

The school's unique atmosphere has produced revolutionary ideas in the area of defense, baserunning, and other fundamentals. The interaction with thousands of players of all ages and skill levels has helped provide unique insights into the thoughts of these players, their parents, and their coaches.

This book is for players, coaches, parents, and fans of the game. Pay special attention to nearly one hundred sidebars entitled "Tips for Future Pros" and "Inside Baseball." These two supplements are aimed at advanced players and coaches who want to get deep into the mental side of baseball.

Think Better Baseball will prove to be a useful resource for players who play either for recreation or with an eye toward a major league career. Players of all ages experience problems with coaches, other players, umpires, and parents. Simply dealing with the pressure to perform at peak levels can cause major problems for young players.

Coaches at every level will also find this book to be a terrific resource in their coaching careers. Every coach has had gifted players and poorly skilled players, coachable and uncoachable players. Many of the instructors at the San Diego School of Baseball have had the incredible experience of playing and coaching at the major league level and working with 6- to 18-year-olds at the same time. The insights gathered have produced the philosophies found in this work. *Think Better Baseball* will change the way coaches look at, and feel about, their players forever.

Many parents have had problems with their children during their participation in youth sports. Conflicts with coaches, other players, and so on can cause major psychological troubles for young boys and girls involved in competitive sports. This book will give parents a helping hand as their kids enter the emotional minefield of youth sports.

THINK BETTER
BASEBALL

How Players Learn

Players Learn at Different Rates

Parents and coaches should remember that everyone has a chance to be good at something, but sometimes it is *not* baseball. Some players just never improve their skills much no matter how hard they try. Other players are satisfied with an average level of play. I know, for I have played the same level of golf (lousy) for 25 years—very mediocre and proud of it.

Human beings are not preprogrammed, so they must learn virtually everything from life experiences. Coaches and parents must realize that every player learns differently. There is a huge difference in the way players learn baseball and other skills at different ages. Players with different experience levels will also learn at different rates. Simple genetics also play a huge part. Some players have a difficult time learning certain motor skills. They may be brilliant in school, in the arts, maybe even in some other sports, but baseball might present a special challenge.

At the San Diego School of Baseball in 1979, Hall of Famer Willie Stargell told me that he knew everything at age 21, and at age 30 he felt like he had a lot to learn. As Willie Stargell indicated, players, especially good players, are resistant to change. Making changes in mechanics and other fundamentals requires taking a risk. Because many players are satisfied with mediocrity or maybe just looking good, they may have a difficult time learning and improving.

Players Are Smarter than You Think

Most players are very smart and can learn at an amazing rate if taught properly in the right environment. In 1985, while teaching at the San Diego School of Baseball, I had a group of eight-year-olds on the field for a quick meeting at the end of the day. I was working for the San Diego Padres and had a Padres uniform on that day. I asked if they had any questions and one kid said, "Why don't you guys get rid of Goose Gossage?" (a great relief pitcher who was having his first bad year for the Padres). Before I could answer, a second eight-year-old said, "They can't; he's got a guaranteed contract." Of course a third young player asked, "What's that?" and I thought I was faced with discussing labor issues with eight-year-olds. While I was figuring out what to say, a cute redheaded kid with freckles said, "That means that even if you don't clean up your room, you *still* get your allowance." I have never underestimated an eight-year-old since.

For players who might appear to be a little slow, coaches must understand that a player's intelligence has little to do with his baseball I.Q. The Oakland A's signed a player from a small town in North Carolina, and, as was our practice, we had him fill out a questionnaire about his high school career. His completed form read as follows: "*Name of High School:* West High School"; "*Graduation Date:* Jennifer Thompson" (you see, this is the name of the girl that he took to graduation). This kid was not the sharpest knife in the drawer, but he became a very smart baseball player.

> **Tips for Future Pros**
> If you don't understand what a coach or instructor says, you should tell him or her, "I don't understand; can you go over that again?" This is being smart.

Sometimes, even smart players will misunderstand what you say. When I was the major league pitching coach in Houston, I often visited the minor league clubs on my off days. On a trip to Double-A Jackson, Mississippi, I saw then-prospect Todd Jones (who later became an All-Star closer) pitch an inning. After the game, he asked me if there was anything that he should be doing differently. Because he had thrown about 15 pitches and they were all fastballs, I suggested that he mix in a curve once in a while. Two nights later while back in Houston, I received a call from his manager and my friend Rick Sweet, who asked, "What did you tell Todd the other night?" I told him, and he said (laughing), "Well he pitched an inning tonight and he threw 20 pitches—2 fastballs and 18 curves." You must make your instructions very clear to players.

Dealing with Learning Disabilities

Lots of players have learning disabilities. Some experts think as many as one-third of all children have some form of disability, with affected boys outnumbering affected girls four to one. Teaching players with learning disabilities is never a big problem. Kids like this just require special attention and a little more loving care.

Whenever I have a student who is not learning as fast as the others, my first thought is that I haven't done everything that I can. I think too often coaches take the easy way out and say, "He just isn't paying attention" or "He doesn't care." Maybe you haven't taught the player using the right methods or haven't taken the time to explain and teach with enough care.

> **Tips for Future Pros**
>
> Smart players listen to coaches and others, give what they say a good shot, then pick out the things that work for them.

Watch Out for the Lefties

Left-handers can have problems while learning skills demonstrated by right-handed coaches. Be careful not to neglect these special people. They may require an extra effort on your part in order for them to understand some skills. I know how left-handers feel because I am very left-handed.

Patience Is Key

If your child is the worst player on the team now, don't let him or her get discouraged. With hard work, encouragement, and good instruction, two years from now he or she could be the best player on the team.

Self-Coaching

It is said that the best sports psychologist for you is the one inside your head. This is not only true but I feel like the best coach for you is also you. My book *How to Hit/How to Pitch* is a study in this concept.

Nerves Are OK

Many players have admitted to me that they are nervous before and during games. Hall of Fame reliever Dennis Eckersley once told me, "I was nervous every time I pitched." Players must realize that everyone is nervous and that these feelings are normal.

Players have trouble learning to relax and allowing their natural abilities to come to the surface. Some players never acquire this skill and don't become the players that they could be. Issues like pressure from parents with out-of-whack expectations, maturity levels, pressure to earn college scholarship opportunities, and overall self-esteem are huge factors.

Although being nervous is a completely normal reaction in a game situation, techniques such as visualization and positive self-talk can help you control these feelings to some degree.

Visualization and Positive Self-Talk

Every good player uses visualization (forming mental pictures) and positive self-talk on and off the field, during practice, and in every game. Most players use some form of visualization already but don't know how to utilize this mental skill to its full potential. To improve your visualization skills, try following these helpful hints:

- Make sure your mental pictures are of a positive nature (e.g., making a great play or hitting a grand slam).
- Begin developing the skill in a quiet place alone. Soon you will be able to form the mental pictures anywhere, even in front of crowds during a game.
- Practice positive visualization on a regular basis (daily during the season). The more you use it, the better you will get at it.
- Include as many details as possible in the visualizations (places, colors, real people, etc.).

If you find a negative picture entering your mind, say "no," start over, and form a positive image. The visualizations become your personal movies, with everything turning out perfectly. If you are pitching, every delivery feels perfectly balanced, every pitch goes right where you want it, and the hitters never hit it well. If you're hitting in your visualization, then you always see the ball clearer than ever before, take nothing but perfect swings, and hit every ball on the nose. When using the mental pictures for defense, you make every play flaw-lessly, and your throws are right on the money. Positive visualization works in baseball and in every other part of your life.

Setting Goals

Having goals is nothing more than having a plan for success. Goals must be very specific; vague goals like "I want to have a good year" simply don't work. Write down your goals and constantly rework and revise them. In addition to having long-term goals, you should plot your progress through a series of short-term goals. For goals to work and so you can determine whether you are reaching them, you must receive constant feedback from coaches and others. Even with this feedback from others, one of the advantages of setting goals is that it allows you to be in charge of your own life instead of putting it in the hands of some-one else.

Different Types of Baseball Learners

Some players who learn primarily with voice commands and descriptions are called *auditory* learners. These players have to hear even the most basic skills explained in detail in a logical manner in order for them to understand fully. Others are *visual* learners. This group must see skills and other information demonstrated and/or illustrated for them so they can form their own mental picture of how the skill should be done. Still others learn the best when they themselves try to perform the skill. This third type is what I call a *physical* learner.

Tips for Future Pros

Every good player I know in the majors uses visualization on a regular basis. Every successful person that you meet in life will also be a goal setter. If you don't set goals, you don't have a plan for your life.

Adding to the difficulty is the fact that most players learn best by being exposed to at least two or all three teaching methods. The bottom line is that a coach, par-ent, or teacher who uses just one method is missing the opportunity to get the most from the players that he or she is responsible for. A good instructor uses all three methods during each teaching session.

The Auditory Learner

Because it seems that the fewest number of kids fall into the auditory category, I think most coaches spend way too much time lecturing their players. Most kids are bored stiff when a coach lectures about a baseball skill for more than two minutes or so.

Attention Span of Young Baseball Players

(Based on teaching players for more than 30 years at the San Diego School of Baseball and All-Star Softball)

- Ages 5–6   2–3 minutes
  The more animated you are, the better.
- Ages 7–8   4–5 minutes
  Demonstrate the skills and take nothing for granted.
- Ages 9–10   5–6 minutes
  Challenge them with a competition of some kind.
- Ages 11–12   7–8 minutes
  Make each player perform the skill in front of the group.
- Ages 13–15   3–4 minutes
  This age group thinks it already knows everything. I tell them that they won't know *everything* until they are at least 16.
- Ages 16–adult   10–12 minutes

Your presentation must be interesting regardless of the age of your players.

Some lecture is beneficial not only to reach the auditory learners but also to help players develop their visualization skills. When a coach uses auditory teaching, he or she is forcing the player to form mental pictures. This may lead a player to be quite skilled at using visualization later on in life. This ability to form mental pictures is essential to kids and especially athletes.

Recognizing an auditory learner.   Coaches will be able to recognize an auditory learner in a group quite easily. As you begin your lecture, most of the students will have their eyes on you. You will notice a few of the players are looking down at the ground as you begin to talk. Although some could be daydreaming, some are also just auditory learners who are trying to form the mental picture of what you are describing. If you say, "Jimmy, pay attention," you make Jimmy look up, and you have probably ruined his visualization in progress. Now he may also think he is in trouble, so you've probably lost him for a while.

It is easy to find out who are the auditory learners on your team. Get the players together and have them sit down; then start talking about some fundamental. As you are talking for a minute or so, let your voice fade out; the auditory learners will look up immediately. They look up because their primary source of information has stopped coming in and they want to see why.

If you want to recognize the auditory learners from the ones who really aren't paying attention, give a short lecture on any subject. Ask the potential daydreamer a question or two about the lecture. The auditory learner will be able to answer the questions, and the daydreamer will have no clue.

The Visual Learner

This is the most common type of learner among ballplayers. They must see skills demonstrated to fully understand them. You will be able to recognize this type of learner because his eyes will follow your every move as you speak. As you have a meeting with your team, walk around the group as you talk. The strong visual learners will never take their eyes off you.

Helping the visual learner.　If you are talking about a second baseman turning a double play from the shortstop, you might say, "The second baseman runs hard to second, puts his left foot on the base, receives the throw with two hands, comes across the bag, plants his right foot, and steps toward first base with his left foot as he throws." As you are saying this, act out what you are describing so that your players can form a picture of this skill and the required movements in their mind. This is what visualization is. Some people are very good at this, and others struggle with the concept. The more visual detail that you provide in your short lecture, the better. A coach shouldn't lecture about more than one subject at a time; if you lecture on the double play then go straight to lecturing about cutoffs and relays, then hitting, you have lost many of your students. You will have some students still trying to picture the footwork on the double play while you've gone on to hitting. The results of this lecture for some players will be total confusion.

Demonstrations, please.   A good coach should demonstrate each skill that he or she teaches in slow motion. If you do not feel comfortable demonstrating the skill yourself, then you can use a model. You should always practice with the model first to make sure that he or she knows how to perform the skill correctly. It is very embarrassing for the model and can ruin your presentation if you have to correct the player during the process.

Tips for Future Pros

Handouts and other visual material are for your benefit. If you are serious about becoming a pro, you should maintain a library of base-ball books and other instructional materials and refer to them before each season.

If you are demonstrating the skill, make sure that you can perform it successfully. I remember one time I told a group of hitters that while practicing off the batting tee you must "keep the ball out of the air and hit hard grounders and line drives." My face got a little red when I popped up the ball on my first two swings. Some of us older guys watch what we choose to demonstrate.

I use models all the time as a supplement to my own demonstrations. I think in some kids' minds they say, "Sure he can do it, he was a pro." If they see one of their peers do it successfully, that thought might change to "If he can do it, so can I."

Using handouts.   We hand out detailed cutoff and relay booklets so the kids can better understand this part of the game. These illustrations make the teaching of cutoffs and relays much easier for the coaches as well as the students. Every major league organization I know has printed booklets like this and makes them available to all of their players in the majors and minors. Every good college and high school coach should also have written copies of their playbooks (cutoffs and relays).

The Physical Learner

This player must go through the movements of a particular skill in order to grasp the concept. Lectures are OK, demonstrations are helpful as well, but nothing replaces the feeling for a player when he or she actually performs the skill. You will be able to spot the physical learners easily. While you are discussing or demonstrating a skill, they will be just itching to get up and try it themselves.

These types of learners will be trying to mimic the movements while still seated. In fact, they can't wait for you to shut up so they can give it a shot. Remember that this might be the only way for them to fully grasp the subject matter.

After a discussion of a particular skill—let's say fielding a ground ball—show the players in slow motion what you want done, then allow them to practice it as a group as soon as possible. I say as a group because if you call them out one at a time, you may embarrass a student who fails the first time he or she tries a new skill. Let the group get to their feet and go through the various movements together. You and your assistant coaches can walk around and correct each student without drawing too much attention to the ones who have no clue how to perform the skill. If the group is having trouble as a whole, then pick someone who is doing the skill correctly and let him or her redemonstrate it to the group. This will happen a lot, and another demonstration at the right time will give you the results that you are looking for.

Using Video to Teach

Hitters and pitchers should be shown video of themselves at some point during the process of learning these skills. Seeing himself on video is quite an experience for a young player. You can explain hitting and pitching skills and demonstrate the proper techniques, but seeing himself will expedite the process of learning a skill considerably. Watching video will also go a long way in helping a player develop his visualization skills.

Some coaches will tell you that using video is a cure-all for problems. I disagree. Some coaches think that all you have to do is show a player a video of when he is doing well, compare it to one when he is struggling, and the difference will jump out at him. Many times this is just not the case. Hitting and pitching mechanics are so fragile and require such precise timing with such subtle differences that they often can't be seen with the naked eye. Here's a tip: if you are watching a videotape and want to get a different view, look at the image in a mirror and you will see the same swing or

Tips for Future Pros

To have an overall understanding of your swing or delivery, you *must* see yourself on video. Encourage your coaches to use video at every opportunity.

delivery with a whole new perspective (righthanders become lefthanders). I have used this technique and seen things that I was missing when looking at the image straight on.

The Good and the Bad

Some players will go into the video room and watch the bad swings and mistakes over and over. This behavior is very harmful, and I would be careful letting players have full access to videos without your supervision. I once banned All-Star pitcher Darryl Kile from the video room in Houston because of his habit of going in there and looking at all of his mistakes over and over. I don't have a problem with looking at the bad things as long as someone spends more time looking at the good things.

Teaching a Skill Using All Three Methods

As a coach in both the National and American Leagues as well as at the San Diego School of Baseball, I have found that the only way to teach is by using all three methods. If you are going to reach all of your players, you must do the following:

1. Describe the skill.
2. Demonstrate the skill.
3. Let them practice the movements.

This should cover all of your students with normal learning capacities. If your players are still having trouble, do it again, and again.

Repeat the Fundamentals

Don't forget that many players learn slowly and repetition is necessary for them to catch up. Some players who learn quickly might complain that "We already know that," but because baseball is a game of repetition and fundamentals, doing a skill over and over until everyone gets it right is healthy for all concerned.

Parents call me and say, "My son is very gifted; he really doesn't need any more fundamentals." I just laugh inside and try to explain that nothing could be further from the truth.

Sorry, Repetition Is All There Is

If a player doesn't like working on the basics, then he or she is playing the wrong sport. Why is it that big leaguers work on fundamentals for hours a day for six weeks every spring training and during the season? Why is it that every new manager hired says, "We are going back to fundamentals"? As I watch more than two hundred major league games a year as a scout, why is it that almost every close game is lost because of poor execution of fundamentals?

Players may not like working on fundamentals and may not understand what repetition really accomplishes. I have a friend who is a very successful college coach named Bob Vetter. When he asked his son Robbie, who was nine at the time, "How was the baseball school today?" Robbie responded by saying, "Bob Cluck is mean; he made us do the cutoffs and relays over and over until we got them right." His dad explained that this is how you learn and repetition and attention to fundamentals is an important part of baseball. Since hearing that story, I go out of my way to explain this concept to the players and their parents at our schools.

Listen to Your Players

Players may come up with a good idea or two to help themselves if a coach with an open mind is listening. In 1972, I was teaching a 12-year-old pitcher. I was trying to explain that a pitcher doesn't push off the rubber but instead strides easily, lands closed, then rotates his trunk. While I was fumbling for the words, he said, "You mean I kind of fall but under control," and there it was, the phrase that I was looking for in order to describe the movement.

After working with fellow coaches Brent Strom, Tom House, Dave Smith, and others in the San Diego School of Baseball, the descriptions *controlled fall* or *tall and fall* became two of the standard teaching terms for pitching coaches all over baseball, thanks to that Little Leaguer on that field in 1972. I have learned a great deal from the hitters and pitchers that I have worked with over the years.

Why Players Don't Learn Baseball Like They Should

I know that you'll think I'm crazy or too critical, but the fundamentals I see in big-league games stink. It's not that players don't know basics, or that they haven't been taught, it's just that some don't think they're that important. For some, I guess it may occur to them that being a sound fundamental team player doesn't pay as much as having big statistics. You can't take the ability to execute a proper run-down or tag a player properly to arbitration. Isn't it funny that the one thing that players always say they want is to win a World Series and get a ring? Teams win championships with pitching, timely hitting, good defense, *and* sound fundamentals.

Inside Baseball

Go to a game and try to count how many fundamental mistakes both teams make; reconstruct each inning and make note of how many runs are scored because of basic fundamental mistakes. The results will surprise you at every level.

In 1989, while we were both coaching for the Houston Astros, Yogi Berra said, "Baseball would be a great game again if only the players wanted to win as much as the coaches do."

I know baseball is a hard game to play at the top, but it seems that there is less and less attention to basic skills and game situations. I'd like to make it clear that I am not referring to errors or physical mistakes, but because I consider myself a baseball purist, it sickens me when I see botched run-downs, relays, and tag plays because players don't position themselves correctly. The worst part is watching the same players do it wrong time after time. This is not always the coach's fault, for the players are told and they just don't apply the knowledge because it is not important to them.

Listening to the Adults

Almost all players that I see for the first time at the school have no idea how to play the game of baseball even though they are eight or nine and have played for two or three years. They don't recognize game situations and therefore don't react to even the most basic plays, and in some cases they don't even know the rules.

The reason is simple. Just go to a game where really young kids are playing any-where in the country and watch them play T-ball (five- to seven-year-olds). They are not asked to make decisions; they don't watch the ball; they just listen to adult commands. They hit the ball and everyone yells, "Run, Billy, run." He gets to first and then looks at the coach who says either "Stay here, Billy," or "Run to second, Billy," and he obeys. This way Billy never learns to advance to the next base because of where the ball is and what the defense is doing with it; he just runs to second because the adults said so.

One issue that gets in the way of players five to seven learning baseball is the fact that some kids never get a chance to play the infield. In an adult-domi-nated T-ball game, the ball is hit to the shortstop and the adults begin telling the shortstop where to throw the ball when it's halfway to him or her. Let's say that there is a runner on first and there will be a force play at second. If the adults didn't say anything, then the shortstop would have to make a decision about where to throw the ball. If the second baseman remembers to cover the base and the shortstop throws to second, all is well. If the shortstop turns to throw to second and the second baseman is not covering, he or she will probably throw the ball to first. Results are as follows:

- The shortstop will learn to remind his teammates (the second baseman) where to be before the play begins.
- The second baseman will learn to cover second next time.
- If the adults don't say anything while the play is in progress, then all of the players can learn from this set of circumstances.

In my opinion, the proper way to coach this age group in this circumstance is to point out immediately after the play that the proper play was at second, the second baseman should cover second on balls hit to the third-base side of the field, and the other players should talk and help out their teammates. In base-ball and in life players need to learn to make their own decisions and be held accountable. They will never learn when all of the decisions are made for them. The result: eight-and nine-year-olds who don't know how to play yet. Coaches should rotate positions in T-ball so that all kids can learn the game properly.

Controlling Coaches

To some degree, substandard coaching may go on for years in youth baseball and beyond. Some high school and college coaches insist on calling every pitch of the game for the catcher and pitcher. These control monsters just won't let the kids think for themselves and learn the game of baseball. Many players, especially pitchers and catchers, come into pro ball or go into the real world unable to think for themselves.

Tips for Future Pros

If you are a high school or college catcher, ask your coach to let you call the game at least part of the time. This is the only way for you to learn how to work and set up hitters.

If I had a son, I would never want him to play for a controlling coach. The best high school and college coaches make their players think for themselves, teach them, and hold them responsible for their decisions. These coaches turn out smart players who make better players and more successful people in general.

The Difference Between Great Athletes and Great Baseball Players

Today's players are faster, stronger, more athletic, and just better than ever before in the history of the game. The problem is some players with outstanding physical tools are promoted through the minors before they have mastered the basic fundamentals. I know that this sounds crazy, but I see some college teams that execute fundamentals better than some major league clubs. Most players are taught these skills but don't execute them when they finally make it. Most major league managers recognize this fact, but sadly I estimate that at least half the players don't care about fundamentals and must be forced to work on them.

Why Players Can't Throw Anymore

Although there are more major leaguers throwing 90 miles per hour than ever before, the average kid playing baseball at the high school level has decreased velocity and accuracy. Players can't throw anymore because of batting ranges. Now I like the ranges, but players need to throw a lot more to develop arm strength. I know this sounds like "my generation was better" stuff, but here goes: when I was a kid there weren't any batting ranges, and there were no pitching machines. If we wanted to hit (and what kid doesn't?), we had to throw to ourselves. It went something like this: three kids went to a park with one or two baseballs. Player one was the shagger, player two was the hitter, and player three was the pitcher. The pitcher threw a pitch, the hitter hit it, and the player way out by the fence caught it and threw it all the way back to the pitcher in the air if he could. The result was more throwing than hitting and lots of fielding practice along with the hitting. Today, many players don't want to work on defense and throwing. Everyone just wants to hit. Too often a team practice is just going to the batting range and hitting, and now they don't even have to pick up the balls. That's why kids today can't throw well, because they don't throw enough—quite simple, really. Kids today are smarter, stronger, and faster, but I see weaker and weaker arms every year.

> **Tips for Future Pros**
> The only way for you to develop your arm is to throw. If you are not on a throwing program similar to the one described in Chapter 4, you will not have a strong and accurate arm.

Why American Players Aren't as Good as They Used to Be

More than a quarter of the players in the major leagues are from outside of the United States. The Dominican Republic provides nearly 10 percent of all the players in professional baseball; Puerto Rico contributes nearly 40 big leaguers and Venezuela more than 30. Altogether, there are players from 16 different countries playing in the bigs.

Baseball is played in the Dominican Republic and many other countries a little differently. Players of all ages have to throw to each other if they want to hit. There are no batting ranges and very few pitching machines even for high school players. Kids play on the sandlot without adult supervision and learn to play by watching the ball and making decisions. When I managed the Las Vegas Stars (now called the 51's) Triple-A team in the 1980s, my smartest player was Ozzie Guillen, who grew up in that environment. He was a 19-year-old shortstop from Venezuela playing in a league of 25- to 30-year-olds, many of whom had been to the big leagues. He just understood how to play. He knew the game situation at all times and helped his teammates to remember what their jobs were. It was like having a coach on the field. He went on to play in the majors for more than 15 years and was considered a very smart major league player. I think that Ozzie and a few other smart players I know—Jeff Bagwell, Steve Finley, Mike Bordick, Scott Servais, Brent Mayne, and Dave Magadan, to name a few—will make good managers and coaches someday.

Coaching—from T-Ball to the Majors

Deciding to Coach

Whether you are coaching in high school, college, or the professional ranks or coaching youth baseball for the first time, do your homework. Read everything you can. This will give you the fundamental base you need. Nobody ever learns everything that there is to know about the game of baseball. Next, get some help, because nobody can coach a team alone. It is a good idea to become an assistant coach first. Even future Hall of Famer Tony Gwynn became an assistant college coach before taking the reins at San Diego State.

Coaching for the Right Reasons

Some people coach because they want to win championships for themselves. Others coach because they think that their kid will get a better shot at playing (a different subject). If you don't really care about the players and are coaching for some other reason, they will know. If you are not prepared at practice or at games, they will know. If you don't have fun and enjoy baseball, they will know. If you try to fool them about anything, they will know. Take whatever time necessary to teach fundamentals to the players you coach. They will have more fun playing when they understand the game situations. In my opinion, the greatest compliment to a coach is that his team is a smart team. Forget the championships won or lost; you are a successful coach if you have taught your players how to play smart baseball.

If you don't have genuine concern for your players and how they feel, you will never be much of an instructor, coach, or manager in T-ball or in the majors. There is an old saying that I love, and we have adopted it at the San Diego School of Baseball and All-Star Softball. The author is unknown: *"Players may not remember what you say, but they will remember forever how you make them feel."*

When You Decide to Coach, You Should

- Make sure the players are having fun on your club.
- Accept the fact that you are a role model for your players.
- Communicate with administrators and/or parents.
- Respect the other coaches and umpires, and behave accordingly.
- Spend time with all of your players, not just the better ones.

Having Fun

I have coached in both the National and American Leagues, and I am convinced that the managers who create an atmosphere of fun, with love and respect for the game, get the best results.

Art Howe is a manager I respect. He lets the players play. When I coached for him, he had a knack for letting the players relax and have fun playing baseball. There is enough pressure, and this philosophy always got good results. We used to laugh, "It's only a damn game; let's have fun and do the best that we can." I remember Art going to the mound and changing pitchers with the bases loaded and no outs. When the reliever arrived from the bullpen, Art would hand him the ball and say, "This is just the way you like it," and laugh. The pitcher would relax and have a much better chance of getting out of the jam.

Being a Role Model

Whether he or she realizes it or not, every adult is a role model for kids. Kids learn from every experience in life. Even older players or siblings are role models for younger kids. Coaches play a special role because of their impact on young players. When we conduct baseball schools I always remind players of this responsibility. The best players have a special moral duty to act in the proper way when they are around other players, for their behavior is always under a microscope and initiated by others.

Communicating with Administrators and Parents

After being a parent, coaching is the toughest job I've ever had. People second-guess you at every level. If you are coaching in youth baseball or high school ball, the parents will say you don't win enough, you don't play their kid enough, or you run your practices the wrong way. But at the same time, they would never offer to help coach the kids. In college and the pros, the bosses blame you for all of the mistakes, yours and theirs, then fire you to save their own skin. In pro ball we get paid well to take that abuse; a volunteer coach should not have to.

Dealing with Other Coaches and Umpires

Coaches should treat umpires and each other with respect. Today you may be winning 10–0 and tomorrow get beat 13–1. Stay humble when you've got a good club; next year you may stink. Coaches have long memories, so don't pop off; just compliment the other club—win or lose—and move on. Remember that players have big ears. Things you say in the dugout or any other time will be taken literally and passed on. Treating others in a professional way makes coaching more fun.

If you keep a good relationship with other coaches and managers, they will also help you beat them. Coaches love to talk about their own players—how they have improved and the things that they are doing well lately. All of that information helps you win. In professional baseball we are constantly searching for an edge. At any level, all information is helpful.

Spending Time with Your Players

The best managers don't give lots of motivational speeches but hold endless one-on-one talks in a variety of places. You may walk all the way out to center field during batting practice to let a player know that you are on his side and are pulling for him. This kind of communication goes a lot further than holding court with the entire team. It is said that the great managers do most of their managing in the clubhouse before and after games.

What Some of the Best Professional Managers and Coaches Taught Me

I played and coached for some managers who were difficult to get to know, hard on the players, and very demanding, but these men had true feelings and tried to be honest and fair. Most big-league players will tell you there are three very big items they find in a good manager: fairness, honesty, and consistency. Baseball is full of people who kiss a player's butt when he's doing well and ignore him and even talk behind his back when he's in a slump.

Manager Joe Torre says, "I try to understand what motivates other people." This philosophy works. Legendary manager Gene Mauch once said that it is much harder for one manager to understand 25 players than for 25 players to understand one manager.

Just Be Yourself

I coached for Astros manager Bill Virdon during spring training and the regular seasons of 1979, 1980, and 1981 while permanent pitching coach Mel Wright was battling cancer. I not only got to be around some great players like Nolan Ryan, Don Sutton, Joe Niekro, J. R. Richard, Doug Rader, and others, but I learned from one of baseball's best fundamental teachers, Bob Lillis, and pitching legend Roger Craig while I was still in my twenties.

Bill Virdon's style was gruff, as he prided himself on being a strict disciplinarian. I was scared to death of the man, at least at first, and so were some of the players. I later discovered that under the surface, he was a caring, wonderful man who had respect for players and for baseball. These are the qualities that I didn't see at first, for he kept his human side concealed for the most part.

One season, we were chasing the Reds and were entering into the final week of the season. During an important game in San Francisco, a drunk wearing a Reds cap kept coming down between innings and yelling into our dugout, "Astros, you are crap; Cincinnati's gonna kick your butt." This went on for the last seven innings during our last game in Candlestick Park. It was funny to me, but nobody laughed in Bill Virdon's dugout in a pennant race. We just called the guy "the drunk." We traveled on to Atlanta that night for a doubleheader the next day. My pitching staff was pummeled; we lost both games, and our pennant hopes were destroyed. After the game, I was sitting in front of my locker feeling sorry for myself when Virdon sat down next to me and put his hand on my shoulder. I thought he was going to let me know how bad my pitchers were and that I would not continue as pitching coach. Instead he smiled, told me what a good job I had done, and said, "Well, I guess the drunk was right." I've often thought that if he had shown this friendly, warm side more often, he might have gotten even more effort from his players.

Motivation

Companies outside of baseball all over the world are now spending more money than ever before to motivate employees, although there is no evidence that it even works. How sad that people hired to do a job must be bribed to do it effectively.

Not all big leaguers have respect for the game, and not all give all their effort every night. I must admit that I get tired of watching some guys play lazy baseball. I believe that at least a third of the players in the majors don't care about getting better. Mediocrity is rewarded handsomely, so some just try to exist, build time in the majors, and not make anyone mad at them.

Baseball players shouldn't need to be motivated. If you have created an atmosphere of hard work and fun, players are self-motivated. I think that this is true at every level.

Players shouldn't need to get up for a game. Pro players should be self-motivated because they are playing in front of crowds and they are doing this for a living. Heck, most young players can't even sleep the night before the game. If anything, they need to come down a little before a game to play their best. Young players certainly don't need coaches or parents telling them, "Well, this is the big one today; you win this and we go to the playoffs."

Tony LaRussa, one manager I respect, has an interesting way to motivate players and prepare them to meet the challenges of a pennant race and playoffs. He puts pressure on his players daily with the feeling that if you pile it on every day, then "pressure becomes your ally," and you outperform the competition when it's crunch time.

"Most horses run fast if you just show them the whip."

—Former Pirates third baseman and minor league manager Don Hoak

Nervous Coach, Nervous Players

Players take on your personality, and if you are running around uptight and hyper, they will have a tough time relaxing. One of the biggest problems for coaches at all levels is getting players to relax so that their natural ability can come to the surface. Enthusiasm, a big smile, and a little humor will do a lot to help players relax. Good managers like Art Howe create an atmosphere that encourages fun and enthusiasm. One year in Houston, we went out of our way to keep utility man Casey Candaele on the club because of his presence in the clubhouse. He kept everyone loose and was fun to have around. In addition, he turned out to be a very good player for us.

Engage Your Players

In my opinion, you need a good personality to become a good instructor. Most people are lousy speakers. Speaking with a monotone voice and little energy in your presentation are surefire ways to fail as a baseball instructor at any level. If you act bored, quite naturally your players will be bored too. I know you are thinking, "Sure, they listen to you, you are a pro. I'm just a high school coach, or just a dad; they won't listen to me." That's the biggest crock. I know coaches with no playing experience who become terrific teachers. They know the subject matter, they like what they do, and they have enthusiasm. On the other hand, I have had a couple of baseball superstars at our school who were big flops with the kids. Why? Because they acted like they didn't want to be there. The kids were bored stiff after the superstars opened their mouths. Many more stars like Alan Trammell, Tony Gwynn, Dave Smith, and Steve Finley are great teachers because they like what they do and the players can tell.

Keep Your Instructions Simple

It is my experience that the simplest solution to a problem is usually the best solution. Although baseball can be a complex game, mechanical solutions to problems in the middle of the game are best addressed in very basic terms. I learned this the hard way. When I was a young instructor, I had a tendency to be too scientific and technical.

One year when Yogi Berra was a coach in spring training with us in Houston, the pitcher was having problems getting the ball down. After he walked two straight hitters with high fastballs, it became obvious that something was wrong mechanically. While I was trying to figure out what to tell the pitcher if I made a trip to the mound, Yogi leaned over and said to me, "Why don't you go tell him to throw it lower?" Because I didn't have another solution that made sense, I went to the mound and told the pitcher just that. It worked, for he threw a low fastball and got a double play, got out of the inning, and went on to win the game. Believe me when I say that I learned from that experience. I learned a lot from Yogi Berra.

Loyalty to Your Players

When former All-Star Dave Smith was the major league pitching coach for the Padres, he once put his job on the line when an impatient general manager and manager wanted to send one of his pitchers down to Triple-A because he was in a pitching slump. Management backed down and kept the pitcher, and he not only made every start of the year but also led the club in wins. The pitching staff wanted to lift Dave on their shoulders and carry him around the field because he displayed that kind of loyalty to one of his pitchers. That is what I call leadership and standing up for what you believe in.

Coaching in Higher Baseball

High School Baseball

Players at the high school level play baseball for a variety of reasons. Some continue to play because they have always played. Others play for the possibility of college scholarships, and others are playing because they enjoy the game. This age group of young men is hard to motivate and to get excited about anything except cars and girls. If I were ever a high school coach, I would keep the ones who loved the game and had good attitudes and would get rid of the rest. If coaches would adopt this policy, they would enjoy their lives more and probably win more games in the process.

College Baseball

College coaches must win to keep their jobs, but most are truly concerned with their student-athletes playing ball and getting an education in the process. Players in their late teens and early twenties are easy to coach. They have all been successful in high school or they wouldn't be in a college program. Most are—at least in their minds—professional prospects and are self-motivated; they realize that it is time to get serious and make something of themselves on and off the field.

The Minor Leagues

Minor league managers can get caught in a professional trap or two. Some are too concerned with which job they are going to get next instead of doing the job that they have been hired to do (teaching and developing players). Inexperienced farm directors put too much emphasis on winning and too little on developing players for their major league clubs, which provide paychecks for everyone in the organization. Farm directors who have this approach are striving to win awards in order to advance their own careers. Administrators like this are looking too far ahead professionally. Players in the minors have no union and no legal rights, are for the most part paid poorly, and are kept hungry to theoretically motivate them. I think this concept is silly. Every smart organization rewards minor league managers for advancing players to the next level rather than for winning championships. Players don't need to learn how to win to become big leaguers. I know many great major league players who were never on pennant-winning clubs in the minors. The biggest mistake that professional baseball makes is to advance players from level to level without making them earn their advancements. This practice produces spoiled, self-centered players who are problems for major league coaches, managers, and general managers.

The Big Leagues

Major league managers have to win, period. Even small-market clubs with small payrolls and no chance to win have to win anyway. When I was working for the Montreal Expos, we had absolutely no chance to win the pennant; the players knew it, the general manager knew it, the manager and his coaches knew it, and I think the fans must have known it because they didn't come to the games. Everyone knew it except the owner of the team. Many owners have unrealistic expectations simply because they don't know the game of baseball. In professional baseball, a little honesty wouldn't hurt the game a bit. Fans and others aren't stupid, and they don't like to be lied to. If you are rebuilding, say so. Most fans will appreciate your candor and support the team during the process.

Support from Above

If a coach or manager doesn't have the support of the people he works for, he is finished before he starts.

With the Astros, I worked for Bill Wood, one of the best general managers ever. He pulled off two trades that will go down in history. He first traded Glenn Davis (who quit a year or so later) to Baltimore for Steve Finley, Curt Schilling, and Pete Harnisch, who all played in All-Star Games. He also traded aging reliever Larry Andersen for a Double-A prospect nobody knew named Jeff Bagwell, who will hit 500 home runs and will enter the Hall of Fame someday. When the Astros were on the verge of being a champion, the new owner fired Mr. Wood, manager Art Howe, and all of the coaches. The next group came in and took credit for Bill Wood's genius. After the 2001 season nearly half of the hitting coaches in the majors were fired. I guess they have to blame somebody.

How the Best Prepare in Advance, and What You Can Learn from It

Every major league club has an advance scout who travels one step ahead of the team at all times. This superscout is a workhorse, and depending on the manager of the big-league club, he may be overworked and/or underappreciated. Managers like Buck Showalter and Tony LaRussa are obsessed with details and information. Others like Bruce Bochy and Art Howe use the information that the scouts provide but rely just as much on their coaches and their own instincts.

The advance scout stays one jump ahead and scouts the team that his team will play next. He writes down where hitters hit the ball, which pitches or which locations of pitches are more likely to get each hitter out, and which hitters are aggressive on the first pitch. Some are first-ball or first-fastball hitters, and some will rarely swing on the first pitch no matter where it is. Some hitters always pull the ball on the ground but hit to all fields in the air. Others protect the plate with two strikes and can be jammed by fastballs inside when behind in the count, while others will swing at a breaking ball in the dirt with two strikes.

The advance scout will chart every pitch to discover which sequences of pitches the pitchers use on a regular basis. Some pitchers will throw a fastball inside then almost always follow with a breaking ball away. Others will back up the fastball inside with another fastball inside. The scout must notice which pitches the pitcher throws, how his fastball moves, how his breaking ball breaks, and what trick pitches he has.

A good advance scout can help to win games.

On every level, you can prepare for games in advance, just like teams at the major league level. If you can't spend any time scouting opposing teams, recruit players and parents to volunteer as advance scouts. If you're lucky enough to have volunteers working as part-time "scouts," here's what they should look for:

Inside Baseball

Next time you attend a major league game, look behind home a few rows up and you will see several scouts with radar guns and notebooks working away. They will carry on conversations about the game, golf, politics, you name it, and never miss a pitch. These major league scouts also begin discussions among themselves that eventually end up in trades between teams. Every team employs scouts that cover every professional team at every level from rookie to the majors. Pretty good job, huh?

Trick plays and other stuff.   Defensively, every team has specific bunt plays and basic pickoff plays. An advance scout must find out if the team has any new trick plays. Even though he has a relatively short look at the team (usually just three days), he has other resources. He talks to other scouts for other teams that are in town, he contacts the local media that he may know, and he is always working the phones and reading publications to stay current on the teams that he is responsible for.

Every manager in the majors is presented a detailed report indicating the lifetime matchup between the hitters and pitchers in the big leagues before every game. Many times managers use this information to set each day's lineup as well as to select the pinch hitters and relief pitchers he will use during the game. Sometimes, when only a few at-bats are used as the base, the information means nothing. When there is a long history between hitter and pitcher, the information can mean a lot. I've seen hitters who were 10 for 12 lifetime off a certain pitcher and 1 for 30 off another pitcher.

Stealing signs.   Every good scout is always trying to steal signs from the opposing teams. We watch the third-base coach and try to pick up which system he is using. Most of us have not only played professionally but have managed and coached and have used many different sign systems ourselves. Most coaches use an "indicator," which is a place they touch to alert the player. The "live" spot, or the spot that means something in particular, will usually follow the indicator.

Regardless of the system, if a scout is lucky enough to get a team's signs, this information will surely help in winning games against that team.

Making the Rules

If you are a high school, college, or minor league coach, make as few rules as possible, but mean what you say. Try to be as flexible as you possibly can, but don't use flexibility as a license to enjoy selective enforcement. When you apply the rules differently for different players at these levels, you will lose the respect of your players. In the majors, managers are forced to compromise and treat stars differently. Players with huge salaries carry a lot of weight with GMs and owners. If you decide to coach youth sports, get everyone together—yes, the kids and both parents—and explain the rules. Don't take no for an answer. If certain parents can't come, then arrange a special meeting for them. If you are smart, you'll make it so their kid can't play until they meet with you; it's that simple.

Whether you are coaching in Little League or in pro ball, meet with the players and explain the rules you expect them to follow. Then give them your rules in writing. If you are a youth league coach and should decide to have as one of the rules "if you don't come to practice, you don't play—no exceptions," then be sure that you are able and willing to enforce it. Your league might have a rule that every player must play three innings. Make sure that you are willing to enforce the rules for everyone, including your best pitcher and other star players. If your rules indicate that a pitcher won't pitch if he doesn't come to practice, then you mustn't allow him to pitch, even in a championship game.

Getting Tough or Being a Good Guy

Please don't make the mistake of starting out easy or being a great guy and then trying to get tough. This is a road to nowhere. The players will lose respect for you for being inconsistent. Instead, start out fair and remain fair and consistent, and your players will respect you the entire season and for years to come. Give them little rewards as they play better and deserve it. Don't try and be buddies with your players. You are their coach, not their pal.

Even Pros Need Discipline

In 1983, I was the director of player development for the San Diego Padres. Four key players on our Double-A Beaumont club displayed poor judgment and destroyed a hotel room in El Paso during the final week of the season. Although we were entering the playoffs, I suspended the four for the remainder of the season. Manager Jack Maloof and the owner of the team supported this decision, although the media and members of our front office were very rough on me. The team won the championship without the four players, and everyone learned a lesson (I hope). When you have rules you have to mean what you say.

The Best Players Should Live by the Same Rules

Your best player may think he's deserving of special treatment. He's not. Most of the good ones don't want special treatment. Some of the amazing stories around baseball are about superstar players getting off the team plane and climbing into a limo instead of riding with their team to the hotel. How's that for being a "team guy"? When I was a coach in Oakland, Mark McGwire was our best player, and he was just one of the guys. He didn't want to be treated any different. I never saw Jason Giambi, Jeff Bagwell, Mike Scott, Craig Biggio, or Nolan Ryan get in a limo when we were all riding a bus.

I've been fortunate enough to be around a lot of great stars who didn't want to have special rules. Alan Trammell, Dave Smith, Terry Steinbach, Mike Bordick, and others just want to be part of the team—no more, no less. This is the way it used to be before some players started to consider themselves bigger than the team or the organization that they play for.

Quality players treat everyone with respect—the owner of the team, the clubhouse kids who shine shoes, and everyone in between.

If you are coaching a college team, a high school team, or at the lower levels, you are not doing any athlete a favor by giving him different rules to follow. Your star player will not respect you, the other players will lose respect for you,

> **Inside Baseball**
>
> There is often a fine line between a coach who runs a tight ship, where discipline is used but not abused, and a coach who is a bully. There is never a reason for a coach to yell at his or her team (except encouragement).

and your rules will become a joke. The star player will ultimately become a better player if he is made to conform to team rules and held accountable just like everyone else.

Making Tough Decisions Concerning Your Players

I recommend that you include in your first team meeting a statement along the lines of, "From time to time I will need to make lineup changes and position changes, etc. These changes will be made only if I think that they have a chance to make our team better." These comments reinforce the idea that we are all in this together.

If the players know what the plan is, they will understand when it is time to put a player on the bench, change the batting order, or change defensive positioning; they may not like it, but they will understand.

Treat Your Players Like Professionals

Players deserve to be treated in a professional way. I don't mean that you ask their permission; I just mean that you should tell them about a move before you make it public. You don't need to justify your move, and you should never feel the need to explain all of the reasons for the move to the players.

You should call the player in and remember to always have an assistant with you. You will always be on the same page with your assistant coach that way, and this is how young coaches learn from people with more experience.

Sometimes you have many changes on your team during the season. Cleveland manager Charlie Manuel had 55 different players and 32 different pitchers during the 2000 season. Even a high school coach will have to deal with players who don't make grades, leave school for personal reasons, and so on during the season. Most of the changes that you make will be because of nonperformance, which will be obvious to all except the affected players.

Changing the Batting Order

Every coach has a different idea of how the batting order should be structured. If you decide to tinker with your order, don't just post it. If a player has been hitting second for a long time and you are dropping him down to eighth, call him in. Tell him, "I'm going to hit you eighth for a while beginning today. I think it has a chance to make us a better team." That's it. Don't get into a discussion about the reasons or who is the new hitter in the second spot. Don't make up stuff to make him feel better. Just state the facts and conclude the meeting. You haven't asked his permission or criticized him, but you have shown him the respect of telling him before you posted the lineup. What quality player can disagree or second-guess you publicly when you tell both him and the press that this move was "for the good of our team"?

If you make the mistake of telling the media and others that you moved him down because he wasn't working the count and getting on base enough, he will naturally ask himself and others why you didn't tell him that. Tell the player, the media, and others exactly the same story.

Moving a Player in the Defense

No matter what the move, somebody will feel that he is being demoted or that he failed in some way. When moving more than one player, I recommend calling in both players (lets call them Smith and Jones) with an assistant present and getting straight to the point. "Smith, I am moving you to second base and beginning today, Jones, you are going to play shortstop for a while. I feel that these moves have a chance to help our team win." Give no definite time frame, no promises, just an honest statement that is short and to the point. This should be the end of the meeting.

Notice the use of "our team" and "have a chance." These subtle references indicate that we are in this together and that you may not have all the answers but you are the boss and make decisions for the common good.

In Houston in the early 1990s, Craig Biggio was our catcher. He and I didn't get along very well at first. Because one of the most important relationships on a club is between the catcher and the pitching coach, I felt that he should be moved to another position, and I was vocal in our staff meetings on this point. I really don't think that anybody agreed with me except Bill Wood, the general manager. Craig certainly didn't like it at the time. Well, we moved him to second base, where he became a star. As is common in baseball today, everyone likes the move now and will say that they agreed with it at the time.

Putting One Player in the Lineup and Another on the Bench

This is a tough one, and I recommend that you see the players separately. Call in the one who is going to the bench, and let him know that you feel that to help the team somebody else should play his position for a while. Explain the things that the player needs to work on, and make him feel that you are there for him and will work with him on these deficiencies. Again, don't get into a long discussion, but get to the point and give him the facts. With the reference to "for a while" and "the team," you have left it open-ended and reinforced the "we and us" concept.

Next, call in the player who is getting into the lineup and tell him of the change. Explain that this isn't a one-game thing but he is to play "for a while" to try and help the team win. If you leave out the "for a while," he may think that he has to get four hits the first game in order to keep his job. I recommend that you explain in detail what you expect of him in his new role and give him a chance to ask questions in this area.

Problem Players

Some players have gigantic egos and will complain about everything. They may not like to take directions of any kind from people in positions of control. They may talk behind everyone's back and second-guess every decision that the coaches make. After a move has been made and things go bad, he may tell anyone who will listen how wrong you were. The problem is that if the player is a veteran player, others will listen. He can destroy your relationship with the rest of the team. Again, make sure you have the facts, and then act.

If he is an average to below-average player, bring him in and discuss the problem face-to-face with your assistant coach present. Lay your cards on the table. Hit him between the eyes with it. The discussion should go like this: "I've heard that you are second-guessing me, complaining a lot, etc. If it is true, I want

Inside Baseball

Watch when a coach or manager goes to the mound. If he knows what he is doing, he walks out quickly with the decision already made. If he is going to take the pitcher out, he should walk with a bounce in his step and signal as soon as he leaves the dugout. A coach who walks slowly and arrives at the mound undecided leaves the impression that he can't make a decision. Good leaders make up their minds and accept responsibility for the outcome.

it to stop. If it is not true, then I apologize for wasting your time." Pause and give him a chance to respond. He will most likely deny it with a response like, "Coach, I would never do that. I'm a team guy. I'm really happy here. Who would tell you something like that?" Ignore the effort to find out your sources, and just say, "Well, I guess I got the facts wrong. Again, I'm sorry for wasting your time." Don't go into details, for there is no way to make this discussion productive. He will never admit he is guilty. This is not his style, for he talks behind other people's backs and hides in the shadows. Did you really expect him to say, "Yeah, I don't like the way you manage, and I have second-guessed you at times"? Don't prolong the discussion, for it can go nowhere.

> **Inside Baseball**
>
> Some big-league managers don't have the opportunity to hire their own coaches, and this creates many problems. Some coaches are pipelines to the office, that is, they tell the general manager everything that goes on in the clubhouse. One coach was called "fifth floor" because the offices were on the fifth floor where he spent all his time hanging out with the bosses and stabbing the manager in the back.

You can't please everyone. Forget any notion that you have changed or will change this individual. He may not be as vocal in his criticism or may not be quite as destructive, but he will remain a cancer. He is going to get worse in some cases as he tries to find out who said these terrible things about him. He will become a bigger pain in the days to come. Get rid of him as soon as possible.

If he is a very good player, I think that you should deal with him in a different way. I know this goes against the Vince Lombardi disciples of the world, the "my way or the highway" guys, the "one set of rules for everyone" coaches, but in higher baseball there are two sets of rules, and that is just the way it is. Every situation is unique, and you must remain flexible yet firm. For a really good player, you still have the meeting, you still say the same things, but you don't get rid of him. You just watch him, ignore him, and live with it for the good of the team. If you are a professional manager or coach (getting paid), it comes with the job. If you expect to win, there is simply no other way.

The Best Have Problem Guys

Do you think for a minute that even the best managers in baseball like all of their players? Dusty Baker managed one player whom he couldn't stand. Tony LaRussa has had a couple in his 20-plus years. And Art Howe (who gets along with everyone) managed one guy in particular who was a despicable person, and he handled the player so that nobody knew that Howe couldn't stand him. These fine managers have a knack for winning over the problem guys by outsmarting them. They give them some latitude and talk with them one-on-one about expectations and respect. It works. None of these great managers would ever admit it and discuss something like this publicly, but it is just something that you live with at the highest levels if you are a professional. In my opinion, there are 10 or 12 really bad guys in major league baseball, not bad out of 750. That is better than the general population.

Coaching Your Worst Player

Players develop at different rates, and a little patience goes a long way. Some of the best players in the majors had rough beginnings. Your worst player needs more attention than anyone else does. Other players will notice and in turn respect the player for his effort if not for his God-given ability.

Andruw Jones hit just .221 in his first year in pro ball and batted just .217 in his first year in the bigs. He started as a sloppy fielder and then in the season of 2000 had 449 total chances (fielding opportunities) and made just two errors. Chipper Jones hit .229 in his first year in pro ball and made 56 errors in 1991 while playing for Macon, but he became a solid big-league player in every way.

Early in their major league careers, Tom Glavine was 2–4 with a 5.54 earned run average and Greg Maddux was 6–14 with a 5.61 earned run average. Now it looks like both are headed for the Hall of Fame.

For a coach, watching a player accomplish a skill that he has formerly been unable to do is one great feeling. I have had these emotions with six-year-olds and with major league players. Many times I may have used the same fundamentals teaching both, with just a different approach for the individual student. Remember that almost all players of all ages have two things in common: they want to improve as players, and they want to have fun.

We Are All Lousy Scouts

I've seen so many players over the years (more than 20,000) at the San Diego School of Baseball and in clinics all over the world. Most of the players continue to attend our programs for four, five, or even ten consecutive years in some cases. Watching their development has been a real education and a very unique experience. Players who are the absolute worst in their group one year come back to be among the best in their age group the following year.

I used to be as guilty as anyone in judging players too soon. Not only am I considered an expert on kids in baseball, I have been employed as a major league scout for years, and I have been wrong many times. Scouting a player and projecting his future abilities is a very difficult task even for the experts.

I asked professional managers and coaches what their biggest problems in coaching were.

65 percent told me that keeping the front office off their backs was their biggest headache.

35 percent said that handling players who were their own biggest fans was tough.

44 percent told me that their biggest problem was handling the pitchers.

55 percent said that they wished they could get substitute players more playing time.

22 percent told me that they didn't like dealing with the media.

33 percent told me that they had trouble motivating players late in the season when they had losing records.

10 percent said that they had no problems at all.

90 percent told me that generally, the attitude and work ethic of all the players has slipped in the past five years.

Watch Out for Labels

Parents and coaches who try to label a player as "great" or "poor" too soon will be wrong a lot. I know major league players who were cut from their high school teams. The Phillies' great shortstop in the 1980s, Larry Bowa, was one. Batting champion Tony Gwynn was not even drafted as a high school senior. Dave Smith, who saved 216 games lifetime for the Cubs and Astros, went completely unnoticed until his junior year in college. One famous basketball player was cut from his high school team for being too slow and clumsy. His name is Michael Jordan.

Coaches, give a kid a chance. Don't pay attention just to the players that are good now, but work with all the kids. A year from now your best player may be the same kid you always used to stick in right field or on the bench. Encourage them all, teach them all, and someone might surprise you. Isn't it a shame that every June, 90 percent of the kids playing Little League are told (in so many words) that they are not good enough to be All-Stars and are finished for the summer? Thanks for coming; see you next year. No wonder there is a huge drop-off in participation at age 13 in our country.

We asked hundreds of young players, "What do you work on at practice?"

75 percent said they mostly take batting practice.

60 percent said that the coaches throw and they are really wild.

70 percent said that their practices are boring.

80 percent said that they rarely work on their defense.

Not one player remembered working on run-downs, baserunning, or sliding at a team practice.

Setting Up Practices

Players, especially good ones, like to be challenged. I have gotten lots of results making good players out of mediocre ones by telling them, "I want to work with both of you, the player you are, and the player you ought to be." Players with a fire inside them will take that as a challenge and ask, "What can I do to become better?" Now you have them right where you want them.

Good practices begin with a good plan—one that challenges players to learn the fundamentals and lets them have fun while doing it. The following is a sample two-hour practice plan that we recommend to coaches at every level.

Questions to Ask Yourself Before You Go onto the Field for a Practice

- Are you keeping a checklist of fundamentals to be covered?
- What do you want to accomplish today?
- Do you have today's drills organized so that they work smoothly?
- If you were a player, would you have fun at this practice?

San Diego School of Baseball—Two-Hour Workout
This workout involves 12 players and one or two coaches.
Remember to be organized, and set up before the players arrive.

4:00–4:10 P.M.

- Meet with the players and discuss the most recent game. Be upbeat and happy, and sell the idea that you're happy to be there.
- Make two or three brief points; make sure you make positive comments before and after every criticism, and move on.
- Next, talk about what the players can expect to learn today. Make sure you tell them that they will learn something new at today's practice.

4:10–4:20 P.M.

Have the players get a partner and play catch. Make sure they are all throwing in the same direction (for example, north to south). Here are some points to emphasize:

1. Center the ball on each throw (move your feet).
2. Close off the front side before throwing (see Chapter 5).
3. Aim for the other player's chest.
4. Take the time to get a four-seam grip on each throw (see Chapter 4).

Don't stand off to the side talking with another coach. Walk around and talk to the players; have something positive to say; communicate with your team.

4:20–4:25 P.M.

Organize the drill. Divide players into three groups of four, explain the drill in detail, and walk them through it the first time.

4:25–5:05 P.M.

There are three stations, and each station lasts six minutes; you can go around once or twice or even three times with older kids. The feeders (station 1) rotate to the coach for fundamentals (station 3), the group with the coach rotates to the infield positions (station 2), and the infielders rotate to become the feeders every six minutes or so.

Station 1. (Feeding Station)—Place four players around home plate. They throw grounders (older players can hit them) to their designated partners in station 2: player one to first base, player two to second base, player three to shortstop, and player four to third base. They throw easy grounders at the players and more difficult ones to each side in order to make the players work for each one.

Station 2. (Infield Play)—Each player takes five grounders at each infield position. The infielder catches the ball and returns it to his partner with a good throw. They receive five grounders at their first position, and then they move as a group to a new position. First base goes to second base, second base goes to shortstop, short-stop goes to third base, and third base goes to first base. When a player is finished with his five grounders, he takes a knee, and when everyone is finished, the group rotates together.

Here are some points to emphasize:

1. Center the ball by moving your feet (get in front of the ball).
2. Stay down and work from the ground up.
3. Close your front shoulder before throwing.
4. Take your head to the target.
5. Hit the player in the chest with the return throw or throw it
   in on one hop if the players are hitting fungoes.

Station 3. (Fundamentals with the Coach)—This can be whatever you want it to be. It can change during each rotation. Options include any fundamental like baserunning, sliding, catching fly balls, practicing run-downs, hitting off the tee, hitting off you, playing an over-the-line game (soft-toss), or going over the signs. Use your imagination.

5:05–5:55 P.M.

Play a game situation, talking about and reinforcing the fundamentals of the day. This is a good time to emphasize cutoffs and relays. Create situations that reflect today's fundamentals, and have fun.

5:55–6:00 P.M.

Have a meeting and tell the players how well they did. Don't make a long speech, and make sure you end on time. Whatever you do, stay positive.

Developing Players

Teams are always in the process of developing players. Every team, even in the majors, will have several players who are developing and learning as players. The teaching and instruction should never stop. It is dangerous to instill the win-at-all-costs attitude, even in the majors. If players have this attitude and stop learning and improving, then they begin to celebrate when they win 13–12 because the other club happens to play worse than they did that day.

The performance and potential of players do count when you look at the long term. Most major league clubs don't have a long-term plan, and this practice is not just bad baseball, it is bad business. You will see teams trade their future away by swapping young players for a veteran and a quick fix. This doesn't make either baseball sense or economic sense. Part of the problem is that the majority of baseball's businesspeople don't have baseball experience, and the real baseball people don't have any business experience. To make things worse, they don't communicate with each other.

Little League coaches, other youth league coaches, high school coaches, college coaches, and even minor league managers might think that their only job is to win games; it is not. At every level, including the major leagues, the job is to develop players—both skillwise and as people—and win as a by-product. With so many young players in the big leagues before their time, the teaching and developing process must go on while trying to win. Sadly, most of the people in the front office simply don't get this concept.

If you have coached a player and he is not a better person and a better player because of his experience with you, you have failed as a coach in my opinion.

Youth Baseball Considerations

Why do 70 percent of our nation's children quit sports at age 13 each year? Perhaps it has to do with the coaches. Parents would never think of letting a teacher teach English in elementary school without the proper credentials. People would not hire an electrician to work on their home without a license. Although there are more than two and a half million coaches working with kids in youth sports in America, fewer than half have any formal training at all. Coaches who could do psychological damage to kids for a lifetime are just allowed to coach.

Inside Baseball

Before you decide which high school or college you are going to attend, do your homework. Go to a game, check out a practice, and see if the coach is the kind of person with whom you want to spend a thousand hours over the next three or four years. If he is organized and a nice friendly man, the chances are you will enjoy yourself and learn lots of baseball. Some coaches who win championships don't help their players to be better players or citizens.

Youth baseball should be changed. At the lower levels, there are lots of reasons why players don't learn as fast as they could. I have watched a thousand games in every corner of the country and have some specific things that I feel should be adjusted.

We need administrators who don't just implement existing policies but who have the courage to change. We need coaches who are willing to self-evaluate and make adjustments. Most of all, we need parents who get involved and make meaningful changes. Changes must be made one team and one league at a time, from within.

Kids are bombarded with all of the wrong messages concerning sports. Watch sports on the news tonight. You will see hockey fights, baseball players arguing with umpires, and, oh yes, the latest news about a player somewhere who got in trouble with the law. If we want sports to be the rewarding experience that they used to be, we (the parents) have to make changes in the system.

A National Certification Program

Some experts say that a national certification program is the answer. I would love to see it, but it is just not possible. For one thing, there are too few coaches already, and we can't disqualify many and continue to make youth baseball work. Some leagues are desperately short of coaches for some programs. Some of the experienced coaches would not attend classes because they may not think they need them. They might tell you, "Hey, I've won four championships; I don't need fundamentals." Who would teach the classes? And when would you schedule the instruction so that all coaches could attend? Youth leagues are too fragmented, with Little League, Pony League, and travel or select baseball teams everywhere.

Four Changes That Would Improve Youth Baseball

1. Use a pitching machine below the major league level (see page 41).
2. Do away with All-Star teams. Instead, play a month longer for all of the kids. Then we don't have to tell 90 percent of the kids in June, "You're not good enough; see you next year."
3. Give rewards for attitudes, not athletic ability. Have an "all-attitude team" instead of an All-Star team. Reward nice kids who are team players and improve the most because they listen to coaches.
4. Rotate positions in games so every player gets to play his favorite position. This way, players would learn to play baseball with a better understanding of game situations, coaches would be responsible for teaching baseball to all their kids, and players would enjoy the experience so much more.

Learning from a Little League Legend

Joe Schloss, from San Diego, has coached Little League baseball for 50 years—that's right, *50 years*. Although he has won his share of championships, he has always had his priorities in perfect order. These are some of the rules he coaches by.

- Players must be on time because we plan our games. We know who will play each position, who will start, and exactly which inning the replacements will come in.
- Players must come to practice. We teach baseball during each practice, working on different fundamentals; if you miss a practice, a piece of your game is missing.
- Behavior problems are not my responsibility; they are the responsibility of the parents. But when they are inside the fence, the players are mine, so parents must leave them alone.
- Lazy or unskilled players need more of my attention, and they get it.
- I never discuss statistics with anyone. This is a team game. Everyone plays, and everyone learns baseball. I have no star players—everyone is equal in my eyes.
- I need the cooperation of the parents to succeed, but I never have long conversations with them.
- I treat every player with respect and expect the same in return.

Seven Reasons to Use Pitching Machines Instead of Live Pitchers for All Players Ten and Under (Below the "Majors" Level)

- The pitchers can't come close to the strike zone. Begin a "pitchers development program" beginning at age eight that teaches basic mechanics (see Chapter 4). Reward the pitchers who develop the best control, and draft pitchers separately so everyone has some strike throwers.
- Frankly, kids get bored to death (so do parents and coaches) when every other pitch is a wild pitch or passed ball. Some kids say baseball is not fun because of this experience with eight-, nine-, or ten-year-old pitchers. Coaches keep telling them to stay alert or get in the ready position, and a ball hasn't been hit to them in six games.

- Kids don't learn defense skills; they rarely get a chance to field a ground ball or fly ball and throw to a base. In most games, the players walk, advance, and score on passed balls or wild pitches. Very few balls are put in play over six innings.
- The games last twice as long as they could. Or, some have two-hour time limits, and they can't finish six innings.
- The hitters get frustrated and develop poor habits by swinging at anything they can reach. After walking ten times in a row, wouldn't you?
- Because few balls are hit, players don't learn to run bases; they just advance on wild pitches.
- Kids don't learn game situations and can't execute cutoffs, relays, and so on.

Even when using a pitching machine, you should continue to use a catcher and allow steals and all other game situations. A coach feeds a youth machine (like a Jugs Junior) on the mound and has a "pitcher" there to field his position. Kids stay focused on the game, they develop confidence as hitters, and they learn defensive skills. A player who *believes* he can hit will make an easy transition to the "live pitcher" league.

Coaching in Games

All coaches and managers at all levels must go into each game with an idea of who they are going to start, who will be the replacements at each position, and who they are going to pitch. Your game plan must include which of your extra players need at-bats, which of your relievers need innings, and so on. Knowing who is and isn't available on your club is very important.

Never assume that the other manager is as prepared as you are. You manage your team; don't try to manage *against* the other guy. Do what is best for your club, and don't worry about him.

Handling Pitchers

Most coaches will tell you that handling the pitchers is one of their biggest challenges. Aside from pitch counts (see Chapter 4), it is simple. When you think that the guy in the bullpen has a better chance of getting the next hitter out than the guy in the game, make the change. Although pitchers do have to learn to work out of jams, don't let your emotions control your thoughts. Games are lost every day because managers leave pitchers in too long. A good rule of thumb: when you're in doubt, take him out.

When you go to the mound, have something to say. I used to hate going out there when everyone in the ballpark knows that you are just stalling until the reliever is ready. Use the catcher or another player to stall.

When you need to solve a problem, most of the time your advice will center around slowing down the pitcher, reminding him of the game situation and who is hitting, and possibly offering a suggestion of what to throw. Sometimes you have to improvise and use your sense of humor to relax players.

In Cincinnati, they shoot off loud fireworks out of a cannon when a Reds player hits a homer. In 1991, pitcher Mark Portugal got a lesson in my coaching style. While leading 5–0 in the fifth inning, Mark gave up three consecutive home runs, back-to-back-to-back on three consecutive pitches. Although all three pitches were good pitches down in the zone and away, manager Art Howe said, "You'd better go settle him down." I said, "All of those pitches were great; he's OK." Art said, "Well, go tell him *something*." On my way out to the mound I knew I had to make up something to get his mind off of the homers, relax, and make him focus on the rest of the game. When I arrived on the mound and it was obvious that he was uptight, I said, "Hey Porch, the guy with the cannon called and said for you to slow down a little bit; he can't reload that fast." Well, Mark laughed, Craig Biggio (who was our catcher then) laughed, and Portugal relaxed and pitched four more great innings and beat the Reds 5–3 that day.

Using Your Pinch Hitters

I would be careful not to use your best guy off the bench too early in the game. Most good managers like to use the pinch hitter who is the worst defensively early because they know they won't be putting him in for defense if they happen to get a lead. Whenever possible, save your best pinch hitter and get him to the plate with a chance to either tie or win the game. When you are really lucky is when your best guy hits with the tying or winning runs in scoring position and the other team's best guy either doesn't get up or hits with the bases empty in a two-run game. Again, don't take for granted that the other manager is as prepared as you are.

Don't be in a big hurry to get the pinch hitter out on deck. Maybe the other manager is going to make a pitching change that may or may not change your thinking and your strategy. For instance, if you have a left-handed hitter on the bench who you want to match up against the right-handed pitcher, wait until the last minute to send him up on deck. The other manager may be asleep at the switch and not realize the situation in enough time to get his left-handed reliever up in the bullpen. It's important that the hitter not take all day getting ready either. I have seen many big-league hitters take forever, getting pine tar and stretching, while the other club stalls long enough to get the lefty ready. You are then faced with either using another hitter or letting your lefty hit against a lefty. Timing is everything.

If you in turn are on defense, make sure that the pinch hitter is in the game (announced in the big leagues) before you make your pitching move.

Case Studies—Players and Coaches in Action

Doing the research for this book has been a great experience. While traveling the world for 35 years, I have seen more than a thousand youth league, high school, and college games and have seen many positive and some negative things. These "case studies" have helped me understand how coaches, players, and parents think. The following stories are a sampling of these experiences. You draw your own conclusions.

Playing Up (Haltom City, Texas, 1997)

Justin was a Little Leaguer about 10 years old. He spent the hour before the game watching his friends play on an adjacent field. It was obvious to me that he preferred to be on field two with his friends the same age even though his team was warming up on field one getting ready to play a game in the "majors" division. His father called to him, "Justin, you better get over here boy, the team is warming up." Justin said good-bye to his buddies and walked slowly to field one. I guess because he was walking slowly, his coach yelled (with a derogatory tone in front of several others), "Justin, if you want to play minors, we can arrange that. Now get over here." Justin headed quickly for the field to join the older players. Justin sat on the bench for the first three innings and then was summoned to play right field for the final three. He didn't have any fun playing right field and struck out against a 12-year-old pitcher in his only trip to the plate. I overheard his mother and father talking during the game, and it was obvious to me that they were just so happy that their son was on the "big" field and playing in the majors, whether he played or not.

After the game, Justin met up with his buddies, his parents left (he obviously lived in the neighborhood), and because the games were finished for the day, the fields were empty. He and three friends (from the minor field) played a game of home-run derby (throwing to each other and hitting) on field two. This kid had the time of his life for the next hour as darkness approached. He was really a good player with solid skills in all areas. When they finished and he was getting on his bike for the ride home, I asked him, "Justin, do you like playing in the majors?" He replied, "My dad wants me to play majors; he says that minors are a joke." "How do you feel about that?" I asked. "My dad said that I'd never be any good if I played minors this year." I asked him, "Would you rather play with your friends in the minors?" He said, "I don't like sitting on the bench; I guess I'd rather be playing in the minors." "Why don't you tell your dad that?" I asked, and he said as he rode off, "I think that it was really important to him that I made majors; I didn't want to disappoint him."

Recognizing the Little Things (Dubuque, Iowa, 1975)

I attended a high school game partly for research and partly because a fan at the ballpark told me they had a third baseman who was a prospect. The third baseman was not a future pro player, but I fell in love (professionally) with a coach that day. Billy was a skinny player who was just not very strong. He was several inches shorter than everyone on his team. I remember thinking to myself that he didn't seem to belong on the high school team. He looked OK in practice, catching and throwing the ball and making every play smoothly. Billy couldn't hit. He didn't start the game, but he was on his feet the entire first five innings cheering his teammates on. From his comments it was obvious that he understood the game and was doing his part as a team player.

With the game tied and the winning run on first, the coach (they called him Wally, I believe) summoned Billy to pinch hit. Nobody understood the move at first (comments from the stands), but Billy made a perfect bunt up the first-base line and moved the runner into scoring position. The next hitter singled, and his club won the game. They crowded around the kid who drove in the winning run, and nobody said anything to Billy.

After the game, the coach had a meeting, and I've never heard anybody in my life talk about teamwork and associated subjects like this man. He talked about having respect for each other and working for a common goal. When he praised Billy for his key sacrifice bunt and attitude, I thought I was going to lose it. The look on Billy's face is the reason men like Wally coach.

I left the field late for my own team practice as the manager of the Dubuque Packers of the Midwest League (Houston Astros farm club). I regret that I never met nor congratulated that coach on his approach and contribution to the youth of Dubuque. I have used many of his comments on players that I have coached and taught over the years.

Too Much Advice (San Francisco, California, 1996)

These players were about 13 or 14 and playing in a playoff game of some kind. There was a large, vocal crowd, and the players were very keyed up. The manager coached third and yelled something after every pitch. I have seen a hundred guys like this over the years. The following scenario is very common from the high school level on down.

If the pitch was called a ball, he said "Good eye" or "Way to watch them." If it was a called strike, his response was, "Come on, be aggressive" or "Swing the bat." If the player then swung at a bad pitch, he yelled, "Come on, that was way up here (or way down there, etc.)" or

"What are you swinging at?" Between the pitches, he had several comments for each hitter like "Keep your hands up here" or "You're pulling your head" or "You're striding too far." In addition, several parents were shouting instructions from the stands. One father had a lawn chair next to the on-deck circle and would fill every hitter's head with garbage before he went up to hit.

The hitters were nervous, confused, almost unable to function, and certainly unable to hit. The hitters would change from overaggressive and swinging at anything to afraid to swing and back again in an effort to please the coach and their parents. It was comical to me and sad at the same time to hear all of these useless instructions flow from the coach's mouth. Because his comments could be heard in every corner of the ballpark, it was obvious to me that he was coaching to the crowd, I guess to show them how much he knew about hitting. I wondered to myself if this coach would have been that loud if not for the big crowd in attendance.

Criminal Behavior (Salem, Virginia, 1969)

Abusing umpires is something that goes on all over baseball. I attended a high school game in Salem and saw my all-time worst umpire story. At the conclusion of the game, one of the coaches followed the umpire to the parking lot and, with all of his players looking on, smashed every window of the umpire's car with a bat. Talk about lessons for life. At least someone had some sense, as I heard that he was fired from the high school (big surprise) and that it had not been the first time that he had done something crazy in the name of baseball.

Spoiled Brat (San Diego, California, 1958)

This is a special story to me. The Little League game started at nine o'clock on a Saturday morning. The kids were excited, dressed in their green uniforms with white trim. One 12-year-old was playing first base and had hit a home run his first time up. It was obvious to everyone that this was a gifted kid who was the best player on the field. When he struck out to end the third inning, he threw his bat and grabbed his glove and started toward first base to throw grounders to the other infielders between innings. He was throwing them way too hard, abusing his teammates, and acting like a spoiled brat. Suddenly from the dugout another player came out and assumed the first-base position. This prima donna was sent to the bench for the remainder of the game for his behavior.

I happen to know that this kid learned his lesson that day. He learned from that coach that no individual is more important than the team, that individual accomplishments are not as important as things like teamwork, sportsmanship, and mutual respect. The name of that great coach and mentor was Joe Schloss. The player's name was Bobby Cluck of the North Park Little League.

The Hitter's Brain

The Mechanics

It is next to impossible to discuss the thought process of a successful hitter without first discussing mechanics. I have studied hitting fundamentals and mechanics since 1968. After signing with the Giants as a first baseman and playing a while, I got released from my contract. I signed immediately with the Pirates (as a pitcher this time), but the experience of getting cut from professional baseball as a hitter left me with a burning desire to try and figure out why I couldn't hit at that level. I hit in Little League, I hit in high school, and I hit .361 as a senior in college. I had always hit. Why couldn't I hit in pro ball? I had to find out.

Even when I signed as a pitcher, I was still interested in hitting because my new job was to get hitters out. All through my career I continued to study hitting to get some answers. When Steve Garvey and I cowrote *The Steve Garvey Hitting System,* which we released as a book and in video in the mid-1980s, several things finally came into focus for me. In doing the research for this book, the subsequent videotape, and all my other books, I have spent hundreds of hours with some of baseball's best hitters. I have picked the brains of Ted Williams, Bob Skinner, Tony Gwynn, Alan Trammell, Steve Finley, Jeff Bagwell, Mark McGwire, Jason Giambi, Dave Winfield, Ozzie Smith, Pete Rose, Robin Yount, Joe Morgan, George Brett, Willie Stargell, and many others. Most of these great players had been instructors at our San Diego School of Baseball over the years. I sought out not just good hitters but hitters that I considered the smartest hitters that I knew.

> **Tips for Future Pros**
>
> Smart players ask lots of questions and listen a lot. Ask managers, coaches, and older players who have been successful.

Lots of Different Ways to Hit

I found many different opinions but also many common fundamentals and a wide range of mental skills used by this group. I watched kids like Eric Karros, Ben Grieve, Tony Clark, and other players who were students of ours and had made it to the big leagues. I have talked to hundreds of kids, some good hitters, some not so good, about hitting. What makes good hitters different from those who are just average hitters? Most of the time it is their mental skills.

Inside Baseball

Watch a big-league game in person or on television and note how many different stances and bat positions you see.

Stick to the Basics

In researching my past four books—this one, *Play Better Baseball*, *How to Hit/How to Pitch*, and *Play Better Baseball for Girls*—I have continued the process, arriving at some very interesting conclusions. The one thought that keeps coming back to me is that hitting is the most overtaught, overcoached skill in the world. No single skill in sports is so misunderstood by coaches and players alike.

Coaches do great damage to hitters when they tell them to "step toward the pitcher." Hitters frequently misunderstand this phrase, taking it literally, and gain ground toward the pitcher as they jump to their front foot. When this happens, they lose all leverage and ultimately bat speed and power. Instead, hitters should assume their stance with an equal weight distribution, that is, with 50 percent on the front foot and 50 percent on the rear foot (figure 3.1). When the pitcher prepares to release the ball, the front foot is picked up as 100 percent of the weight goes to the back foot. At the same time, the bat is triggered (put into motion) as the body "loads" for the swing (figure 3.2). A hitter should attempt to pick up the stride foot and put it back down in the same place. Immediately after the front foot is planted at a 45-degree angle to the body (figure 3.3), the trunk begins its powerful rotation (figure 3.4). As the hands stay inside the ball (figure 3.5), the bat is accelerated and hits the ball with a force of several hundred pounds (figure 3.6).

Tracking the Ball

Baseballs have seams to make the flight of the ball stable. It is the same with a golf ball, in that without dimples, the ball would fly out of control. The debate rages on by great hitters as to whether they see the spin on the ball or not. Joe

3.1 Hitters should begin with their weight equally distributed on each foot.

3.2 When the pitcher prepares to release the ball, the weight goes to the backside as the body "loads." At the same time, the hands move back to trigger the bat.

3.3 After the stride foot is planted, the trunk begins rotation, and the hands work inside the ball to begin the swing.

3.4 The back foot pivots so that the trunk can rotate forcefully in order to create bat speed and power.

3.5 The bat is accelerated in the most efficient way when the hands remain close to the body as they come forward.

3.6 At impact, the head stays down in order to see the ball for as long as possible.

Morgan says you do; Tony Gwynn says you don't. Opinions on the subject are split about 50-50 in the world of baseball. I personally think that hitters see the trajectory first and then on some pitches they see the spin. Whatever the case, the last bit of information that hitters get from their "tracking systems" (primarily their eyes) is the speed. This is why pitchers who throw change-ups with the arm speed of a fastball (Trevor Hoffman's is the best) are very effective.

One of the keys to becoming a good hitter is to develop your tracking system to the maximum. Through your eyes, your onboard computer (your brain) gains information about the pitch; recognizes the type of pitch, its trajectory, direction, and speed; and directs your muscles to deliver the bat at the correct place and time in order to hit it hard. Because most fastballs get to the plate in half a second, and because the hitter must start the bat forward when the ball is about halfway in order to hit it, the hitter has only about a quarter of a second to gather a huge amount of information about the pitch. It should make perfect sense that without a still head and eyes, your tracking system can't be efficient, and you have virtually no chance of being good at this difficult skill.

Tips for Future Pros

We estimate that about two-thirds of all young players need some kind of correction or can improve the way they *see* the ball.

Fastballs never rise. Every pitch drops on what is called the "parabolic arc," that is for a fastball at 85 miles per hour (mph) between two and two and one-half feet from the pitcher's release point to home plate. When a fastball is thrown with four-seam rotation (see Chapter 4) it stays up longer or, in other words, drops less. Factors like humidity and arm angle also play a part in the amount of drop. Pitches lose about 6 percent of their speed on the way to the plate. When I set my radar gun on a pitcher at his release point and then allow the gun to "roll down" or get the reading at the plate, it will be about 6 percent less (for example, the reading is 85 mph out of the hand and 80 mph at home plate). Because most hitters swing over most pitches from the waist down, the hitter's tracking system underestimates the amount of drop on the pitch. When the pitch is spinning other than with four-seam rotation, it will drop more because of the drag on the seams (see *Play Better Baseball* for more information). Because the ball is constantly changing speeds as it is affected by the air and gravity does its work, the hitter must continue to make final adjustments with the path of his hands and therefore the bat head.

Good tracking begins with seeing the ball clearly at the release point of the pitcher (figure 3.7). Most good hitters look at either the hat or jersey of the pitcher so that they can focus at the proper distance like the lens of a camera. When the pitcher's arm starts forward, you switch your eyes to the release point, and the ball will appear in clear focus sooner. If you keep your head still and rotate under

3.7 In order to track the ball effectively, the hitter should concentrate on seeing the ball at the pitcher's release point.

a still head, the ball will remain in focus the entire length of its path or all the way to your bat head. Try going to the bullpen when your pitcher is warming up and just practice "seeing" the ball. You can also do this at the batting range every few pitches to help you improve your tracking skills.

Use YOUR Stance

The stance is one of the most overtaught areas. Coaches should let the hitter get comfortable and not be concerned with much else. Hitters should not worry about where they start their hands. Be yourself, for any stance will work if you follow the simple fundamentals outlined here. If you are unsure where to stand in the box, try the basic position that we recommend for young hitters. Measure the distance of one of your feet from the front edge of the plate (figures 3.8 and 3.9).

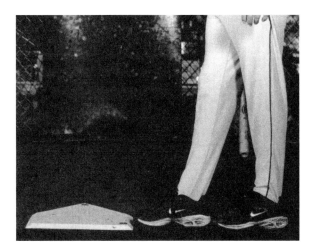

3.8 Determine the proper distance from the plate by measuring one of your feet.

3.9 This distance will provide for both plate coverage and the ability to turn and get to the inside pitch.

This is a good starting spot for almost all hitters. It provides for full plate coverage and yet is far enough to allow you room to get your hands to an inside pitch. The important issue concerning your stance is that you assume the same position in the box for every pitch. Any hitter that moves around in the box from pitch to pitch will never learn the strike zone.

Do NOT Transfer Your Weight

A hitter should keep his head still, begin with his weight divided evenly between the front and rear foot, go to the back foot when he triggers the bat, and return to evenly distributed weight, as mentioned. The trunk then rotates under a still head. A hitter should not gain ground toward the pitcher. When a hitter transfers his weight forward to his front foot, he loses leverage and therefore bat speed and power. Kids are often told, "Step toward the pitcher." I know I used to use this phrase myself and then noticed that it hurt more than it helped. Hitters take this information literally and step toward the pitcher, incorrectly transferring their weight and losing power. Power is increased *not* by transferring the weight forward but by keeping the hands close to the body and rotating forcefully under a still head.

You Want More Power?

If you want to increase your bat speed and power, you should strengthen your abdominal muscles in order to rotate faster. Four great examples of players who have done this are Manny Ramirez, Tony Gwynn, Mark McGwire, and Jeff Bagwell. None of these players take strides at all; instead, they pick up the front foot and put it straight back down where it was. It should also be noted that most power hitters today use a relatively light bat, and Barry Bonds even chokes up on every pitch.

Developing Good Hitting Habits

Don't Be a Pull Hitter

More hitters are destroyed both by trying to pull the ball and by trying to become powerful than by anything else. My favorite saying is, "There is nothing wrong with pulling the ball, but everything wrong with *trying* to pull it."

In 1999, Darin Erstad of the Angels hit more than 130 balls (for outs) to the second baseman and first baseman (he is a left-handed hitter). During that season, as a pull hitter, he hit just .253 and had more than 100 strikeouts. In the 2000 season, he stopped *trying* to pull the ball, used the whole field, and got 240 hits, hit .355, and had 100 RBI.

Getting a Good Pitch to Hit

Being patient at the plate comes with experience and the belief that you can still hit successfully even if you get behind in the count. Some hitters are scared of taking a pitch or two because they just don't believe that they can hit behind or with two strikes. Successful hitters don't get themselves out very often by swinging at bad pitches. The minor leagues are full of hitters who give up one or two at-bats every night by being impatient. It is fine to think of yourself as an aggressive guy, but at the plate you must wait for a good pitch to hit. A veteran pitcher will pick you apart once you

Tips for Future Pros

The best advice a hitter can get is to "let the ball come to you." In an effort to be aggressive, powerful, and quick, most hitters incorrectly transfer their weight toward the ball and reach for it.

get a reputation for swinging at balls out of the zone. The late Tony Pacheco had a great analogy for this situation. He said, "Hitting is liking taking a bus to work: some guys will get on the first crowded bus and stand up for the forty-minute ride, while smart guys wait five minutes for the next bus that has plenty of seats on it and are comfortable all the way downtown." Hitting coaches Keith Lieppman (Oakland A's) and Grady Fuson (Texas Rangers) teach working the count better than anyone. On the first pitch, hitters hit .180; at 2–1 averages go to .340.

Tips for Future Pros

If you think that hitting is something that you can do unprepared, you are fooling yourself. Hitting is a very difficult skill.

Good Hitting Takes Time

Developing as a hitter takes lots of time. The proper instruction, a strong work ethic, and a good practice plan will give you a chance to become a good hitter. Hitting is repetition, thousands of swings the right way before things work in games consistently. There simply is no other way. No other skill requires more practice, more dedication, and better mental skills than hitting. If a hitter develops an efficient swing and a plan for success early in his playing career, he will improve at a terrific rate and reach his potential.

Inside Baseball

Check out the back of a baseball card or the press guide of a big-league team and you will see that most hitters had a tough time their first year or two. Many big-league stars were sent back down to the minors once or twice. Some kids also have trouble at different stages of development.

Don't Wait Until the Last Minute

High school hitters come to us three days before their first high school practice and/or tryout and need a "quick" hitting lesson. They think that if they take hundreds of swings for a few days they can cram for tryouts like they would for a physics exam. Many California high schools have more than 200 players try out for baseball with 14 spots available on the team. The competition is often fierce for freshman, junior varsity, and varsity spots.

Little League parents buy their sons or daughters $200 bats (usually too big) and head for the batting range just 48 hours before tryouts when the kid hasn't hit in three months. That kid cries like a baby when he or she doesn't make the majors level or is not in the starting lineup. Worse, some kids who don't understand the preparation necessary to become successful at any endeavor just think that they aren't any good, lose interest, and quit the game. Although grossly underprepared, kids who fail to make their teams complain that "the coach didn't like me," or the parents will complain that "it was all politics." Welcome to the real world. There are politics in every walk of life, in every company and organization in the world. You can make excuses, or you can be the player that prepares better than the rest and gets the spot on the team.

Your Hitting Schedule

In order to become the best hitter that you can be, you must set up a hitting schedule and follow it. It must be challenging and productive in nature yet be easy enough that you won't scrap it after a week or so. Thirty days before your first practice or tryout, begin your program and stay with it throughout your season.

Four hundred young hitters were asked the question, "What do you need to do to improve your hitting?"

85 percent said they wanted more power.

60 percent said they needed help hitting breaking balls.

35 percent wanted to learn how to pull the ball more.

55 percent said they swung at too many bad pitches.

Only 15 percent wanted to learn to hit the ball to the opposite field more.

Hitting—a Practice Plan for Success

There are really four different stages of preparation to get you ready for the season: shadow swinging, hitting off the tee and soft toss, hitting in the batting cages, and taking live batting practice.

Shadow Swinging

The first stage of preparation consists of shadow swinging using visualization. Simply get your bat and go out in the backyard or another open space. Assume your stance, and focus on an object about 60 feet away. Visualize a pitcher who winds up and throws a fastball down the middle; swing and hit a line drive. You hit nothing but line drives in this drill. Visualization is a powerful tool. (Please refer to Chapter 1 for more details on visualization before beginning this drill.) Take your time and hit 40 balls at the rate of about four per minute. This 10-minute workout gets your hands and arms in shape and gets you ready for the next stage of preparation.

Hitting Off the Tee and Soft Toss—Not Just for Kids

The second stage will require a batting tee, a rubber home plate, and some Wiffle balls. Get in your stance just as you did when shadow swinging. Make sure that you are in the same place in the box every time. Place the tee on the outside half of the plate, and hit the ball up the middle from line drive on down (keep the ball out of the air). Don't move closer to the plate because the ball is away. Stay where you are so that you can practice hitting the outside pitch the other way or up the middle. Next, have another player or coach toss balls underhanded over the plate from the side. This forces hitters to make adjustments to balls up, down, in, and out.

Head for the Batting Cage

Stage three involves going to the batting range. You should always get into a batting cage that is right for you. The posted speeds are the actual speeds of the ball. When hitting off a machine, you must subtract 10 to 15 miles an hour from the speeds you normally face because you don't have an arm to time the release as you do with a live pitcher. In addition, the distance is usually about 42 to 45 feet.

Tips for Future Pros

If you don't like to hit and are not willing to take thousands of swings a month to develop your swing, quit. You will never be any good.

Twenty years ago while setting up a batting range in San Diego, I asked Alan Trammell and Tony Gwynn to hit and tell at what speed they were hitting a big-league fastball. They both said that the 65-mph machine setting simulated the average 85-mph major league fastball. If you are in pro ball and normally face a pitcher throwing 85 miles an hour, you should practice your hitting in a 65-mph cage.

Refer to the batting range chart for the correct speed for you. It does you more harm than good to hit in a cage that is faster than the indicated speed. If you are in a cage that is too fast, you will not trigger (load) the bat properly and will create a premature jump (weight transfer) at the machine. I cringe when I see hitters destroying their swings in a cage that is too fast. People don't understand and they think that they are preparing themselves instead of ruining their swings.

Eight-time batting champion Tony Gwynn hit in our batting cages when he was young and would always hit at 50 mph and never any faster. If you are going to work on your mechanics, you don't need to be challenged in practice. Stay in a slower cage and learn to become a good hitter. When you are hitting in a batting range, hit 10 or 20 balls, then take a 20-second break, stretch, take a deep breath, and then resume hitting.

You should never take more than 50 to 100 swings in a workout. At some point, swinging becomes counterproductive; when a hitter gets tired, he begins to use his upper body (shoulders) to get the bat through and "comes off" (pulls away) with the front side.

A Trip to the Batting Range

Age of the Hitter	Speed of the Live Pitches He Faces	Batting Range Speed
8	40	35
9	40	35
10	45	40
11	50	40
12	55	45
13–14	55–60	50
15–16	60–75	55
17–18	75–80	60
College/pro	80–85	65

Live Batting Practice

At least 10 days before practice begins, grab a teammate and begin hitting off each other. Take about 50 to 60 swings at least three times a week (see the 30-day plan on page 60). Pay special attention to picking up the release point and seeing the ball clearly. Even though the batting practice is slow and it is easy to pull, stay inside the ball and use the whole field. Begin every round with hitting the ball to the opposite field.

When you take live batting practice, you must have a plan. All-Star Roberto Alomar hits every ball the other way the first round and then spreads the ball all around from that point on. This practice locks your front side in and helps you keep your head down and maintain other good habits. Tony Gwynn, Craig Biggio, and many other good hitters have the same kind of routine during batting practice.

You are now ready to go to spring training, your first practice, or a tryout. If you don't prepare, just remember that you will be competing against people who have. If you prepare well and get cut anyway, you will know that you did everything that you could. You can live with that.

A 30-Day Plan to Get a Hitter Ready for the Season

Day	Drill	Details
1	shadow	10 minutes, 40 swings
2	shadow	10 minutes, 40 swings
3	shadow	10 minutes, 40 swings
4	day off	
5	shadow and tee	4 minutes, 16 swings shadow and 24 swings off the tee
6	shadow and tee	4 minutes, 16 swings shadow and 24 swings off the tee
7	shadow and tee	4 minutes, 16 swings shadow and 24 swings off the tee
8	day off	
9	batting range	10 minutes, 40 swings
10	batting range	10 minutes, 40 swings
11	shadow and tee	4 minutes, 16 swings shadow and 30 swings off the tee and soft toss
12	day off	
13	batting range	10 minutes, 40 swings
14	batting range	12 minutes, 50 swings

Day	Drill	Details
15	shadow and tee	4 minutes, 16 swings shadow and 36 swings off the tee and soft toss
16	day off	
17	live batting practice	10 shadows to warm up then 30 to 40 live swings
18	batting range	12 minutes, 50 swings
19	live batting practice	10 shadows to warm up then 30 to 40 live swings
20	batting range	12 minutes, 50 swings
21	day off	
22	shadow and tee	4 minutes, 16 swings shadow and 40 swings off the tee
23	live batting practice	10 shadows to warm up then 40 to 50 live swings
24	batting range	15 minutes, 60 swings
25	live batting practice	10 shadows to warm up then 40 to 50 live swings
26	day off	
27	shadow and tee	4 minutes, 16 swings shadow and 40 swings off the tee
28	live batting practice	10 shadows to warm up then 40 to 50 live swings
29	live batting practice	10 shadows to warm up then 40 to 50 live swings
30	day off	

Hitting in Games

The preparation for each game begins as soon as the previous game is over. It is a good idea to go through a self-evaluation process after each game. Many players are way too hard on themselves and choose to dwell on the negatives. Try to think about the good at-bats and the good things that you did. Every game is full of negatives if you choose to dig deep enough. As a coach, I choose to pick out all of the positive things that each player did in a game and build on them. I believe that each player should adopt this "blue sky" approach. Make note of all the good things that you did and the things that you learned, and reflect on the wonderful opportunity you have playing baseball. The bad things will seem insignificant.

> **Tips for Future Pros**
>
> If you don't believe in yourself when you get into the batter's box, the pitcher will know. I don't know how he knows, but he will know. When you get into the box, act as if you want to be there; project positive body language. It helps.

Pitchers and Catchers Tipping Their Pitches

Lots of pitchers give away their pitches in their gloves. If you watch closely, you may see them get different grips or take a long time to grip their change-ups or splits. Many inexperienced pitchers have a higher arm angle on their curves, and some have patterns on how they shake off (turn down the sign from the catcher) certain pitches on certain counts. Watch closely from the on-deck circle and bench and see what you can see.

Catchers sometimes assume a different stance after they call a breaking ball (to block it more effectively if it's in the dirt). You will see them assume a wider stance or move a little closer to home plate. Sometimes you may notice them taking much more time to arrive in their receiving stance after they call a curveball. Noticing all of these little things makes you a smarter player and hitter. I have also seen catchers set up deeper when they are going to attempt a pickoff at first or third base (in order to clear the hitter with the throw).

> **Inside Baseball**
>
> Try to get into a stadium before the gates open someday. You will see how hard and long the hitters work on tee drills, soft toss, and extra batting practice. It's hard to become a good hitter.

Get There Early and Prepare Properly

Make sure that you have enough time to get yourself ready physically and mentally before a game. If your team is taking batting practice, then make sure you are loose when it's your turn to hit. Make the most of your batting practice by establishing good fundamentals. By hitting the first four or five pitches the other way, you will be working your hands inside the ball. Be sure to keep your head still and keep your balance solid. Don't try to put on some kind of display of power; just get ready to perform in the game. Get your eyes working, see every pitch clearly, and hit every ball you can right on the barrel of the bat. Sometimes when a coach is throwing batting practice hitters slip into what is called a "soft center." In this state of mind, hitters don't pick up the release point of the pitcher and see the ball late in its flight. Because a coach is throwing easy, hitters can get away with it, have a decent batting practice, and think that they are preparing properly.

Ask some questions. Maybe some of your teammates have faced today's pitcher before. Maybe your coach knows something about him. As you play other clubs, ask players on the other teams about pitchers in the league. You should keep a little book on pitchers you face and what they throw.

Watch the opposing pitcher warm up. He will show you all of his pitches and give some insight into what you will be facing. This practice is critical if you are serious about your hitting. While watching the opposing pitcher warm up, ask yourself the following important questions:

Inside Baseball

Watch a game on TV and notice how some hitters try to peek to see where the catcher is setting up (in or out). Players who do this will be warned about peeking by the catcher when they face that team again. Ignoring such a warning could have unpleasant consequences.

- Where is his release point (see figure 3.7)?
- What pitches does he throw?
- Which pitches did he get over the plate?
- Did his fastball move, or is it straight?
- What was the tilt (angle) of his breaking ball?
- Does he tip his pitches?
- What is his best pitch?

Of course you can see the release point of the pitcher when you are on deck waiting to hit, but try to establish his basic release point in the bullpen. Make note of the different pitches he throws. He will motion with his glove and describe the way each pitch moves. Watch and see which pitches he gets over the plate. This may change a little when he gets into the game, but most pitchers have trouble commanding some of their pitches. If you can't see the bullpen from where you are before the game, watch all of the hitters hit before you and study all of these things. Some hitters are not smart enough to watch the game and are not prepared when it's their turn to hit.

Tips for Future Pros

Do you want to look good just in batting practice, or do you want to develop as a hitter and prepare for the game? Have your coach throw you curves and off-speed pitches.

Recognizing Different Pitches

In order to recognize different pitches as early in their flight as possible, you must pick up the release point as mentioned. The quick arm will give away the fastball. Most pitchers outside of the majors slow their arms down on both curves and change-ups. Most high school and college pitchers throw their curves up rather than out, as described in Chapter 4. You will see the ball pop up above the plane of the high fastball immediately after it leaves his hand. Try looking for the fastball all the time, and adjust the best way you can to the other speeds as you learn what to look for off pitchers.

Inside Baseball

When the hitter fouls the pitch straight back to the screen (almost always a fastball), he is right on it. Most times, you will see that the pitcher will change speeds or at least throw a different pitch. The pitcher makes these adjustments from pitch to pitch.

A Plan for the Game

I think that hitters should look for the fastball out over the plate all the time. By looking out over the plate, your front side will stay in, you will watch the ball longer, and you will cover the whole plate. If the ball is in fact away, you are set up to hit it. If the ball is in, you have plenty of time to adjust and get the bat head to the ball. You must trust yourself that you can get to the ball inside without having to look for it. I'm sure that you can see that it would be impossible for you to look for the ball inside and then adjust and hit the ball if it is away from you by reversing your trunk rotation.

Watch the pitcher throw to the previous hitters and begin the process of "eliminating" pitches. For most pitchers below the major league level, it will become obvious that he can't get at least one of his pitches over. For example, if he throws a fastball, curve, and change-up but rarely throws his curveball for a strike, just eliminate it. You should now know that everything he throws is straight (his fastball and change-up). He probably doesn't throw his change-up all that much, so in your mind he is now just a fastball pitcher.

What patterns does he use to get hitters out during the game? Most pitchers have definite patterns. Even accomplished big leaguers use sequences of pitches over and over during a game. The most repeated sequence in baseball is the same from high school to the majors. When a pitcher throws a curveball and misses, he almost always throws a fastball on the next pitch. You can count on it. Some pitchers have no other option but to throw a fastball on counts like 1–0, 2–0, 2–1, 3–1, and 3–2. These are offensive counts, and the edge goes to the hitter. Most pitchers lack the confidence or the courage to throw a breaking ball or change-up on counts like these. Sit on a fastball and take advantage of these and other patterns he shows you. Being patient and working the count will get you to these counts more often.

Inside Baseball

Watch how the starting pitcher changes his pattern of pitching during the second and third time through the batting order.

Start becoming a smarter hitter by watching the game more and learning more about the pitchers that you face and, more important, learning and trusting yourself as a hitter.

Are You an RBI Man?

People who drive in runs for a living have to make certain concessions. Instead of working the count and trying to get on base, hitters in the middle of the lineup should go out of the zone to drive in runs. There are big-league stars who simply won't do it. Jason Giambi, Barry Bonds, and even the great Ted Williams never compromised their strike zones even with men in scoring position. These guys will take their walks and leave the RBI to the next guy. Is this being selfish or showing their respect for the team and the hitters hitting behind them? Players like Edgar Martinez, Manny Ramirez, and Juan Gonzalez are just the opposite in that they will go out of the strike zone to drive in runs. They feel that this is what they are being paid to do. Who is right? I don't have the answer.

Tips for Future Pros

Be honest. Ask yourself the question, "Do I really watch the game while in the dugout between innings?" Good players do.

On-Base Percentage

Earl Weaver used to talk about working the count and making the pitcher work for every out. Many current general managers like to make people think that they invented this concept. When I signed and played pro ball in the 1960s and 1970s, my instructors who had played in the 1940s and 1950s all talked about these same ideas that we hear today from the new group of boy wonders (young general managers).

Tips for Future Pros

Don't let anyone give you take signs on counts like 2–0 and 3–1. Hitters don't learn how to hit by taking fastballs down the middle and trying to get walks. If you are getting take signs on these counts, talk to your coach.

Many hitters get reputations for swinging at everything, and it doesn't take long for the other clubs to catch on. If a hitter has one major hole (an area that he can't handle and swings anyway) or chases pitches out of the zone, the word gets out quickly.

Some hitters are notorious first-ball hitters. Preston Wilson and Moises Alou are two that come to mind. The other extreme was Wade Boggs, who almost always took the first pitch.

A Two-Strike Approach

Every hitter should develop a good approach with two strikes. Some players choke up some, some players spread out a tiny bit in their stance, and others just look for an off-speed pitch with the belief that they can fight off (at least foul off) a fastball. Others look for something away and just react to the ball if it is in. At any rate, you must protect the plate and at least stay alive. Tony Gwynn began his career with a two-strike approach and liked it so much that he used it all the time. He was always one of the toughest men to strike out in all of baseball.

When your club is way behind, your manager may ask you to take a strike at least until the tying run comes to the plate. I never liked this idea much. I think a hitter becomes skilled when he remains consistent from one at-bat to another.

Stealing Signs from Second Base

When many big leaguers are on second base, they watch the catcher's signs and try to relay them to the hitter. Although your primary responsibility is to watch the pitcher and assume your lead, you should have no trouble doing both. The best information that you can relay to the hitter is whether the catcher is setting up inside or outside and not so much the type of pitch. Most hitters will not want the type of pitch no matter how sure you are, for if you make one mistake and signal a breaking ball and it's a fastball in, he may get killed. Early in the count most catchers in higher baseball will not set up down the middle but choose either in or out. If you can let the hitter know where the catcher is setting up, he will have a terrific edge. For instance, when the catcher sets up inside, it is usually a fastball (you don't throw a curve or change-up in). Players will signal by taking a step one way or the other or by touching their hats (too obvious) or looking back at the bag when the catcher sets up on that side of the plate.

Some first- and/or third-base coaches will also steal signs either from the catcher (if he is showing his signs) or the pitcher (if he is tipping his pitches in his glove). They will in turn relay the pitch to the hitter by a whistle or by bending up or down. Again, giving the pitches is rare because it takes only one mistake to get someone hurt. Art Howe is very good at picking up pitchers' pitches, but I have seen many hitters who don't want to know even though he is sure.

I would estimate that at least 20 percent of the pitchers in the big leagues and maybe 50 percent of the pitchers in college tip at least one of their pitches while in their gloves. The most common problem is the tipping of change-ups and splits by flaring (opening or moving) their gloves as they get the grip. Many pitchers now grip their change or split initially and then change to the easier grips after they get their sign.

Head Games

Some players are very superstitious, and hitters are the worst. Some hitters like Jeff Bagwell have a set routine and will never vary from it. Jeff approaches home plate, gets into the box, backs out, turns his back on the field, and takes two practice swings before going back in for the first pitch. Every at-bat, all year, every year, it works for him, so why not? Watch hitters in the box, and you will see the same habits at-bat after at-bat. Some hitters wear pads and other armor that gives them the ability to stand on top of the plate and hit the ball on the outside corner more effectively. This practice gives the hitter a psychological advantage over the pitcher.

Don Pisker was a hot prospect for the Astros who played for me in Dubuque, Iowa, during 1976. Sometimes in the Midwest, there were train tracks near the old ballparks, and Dubuque was no exception. In the middle of an at-bat one night, a train started going by. Pisker stepped out and wouldn't get back in the box until the train passed because it was hurting his concentration. Freight trains in the Midwest can go by for 30 minutes, and finally the other manager got upset and the umpire ordered Don into the box. He struck out and looked really bad. The word got out about this incident, and every team in the league began shouting, "Here comes the train" for about a month. Pisker had a lot of trouble concentrating with this going on and had a bad month. He finally got over it, had a good year, and advanced to the next level in baseball. People will do anything to help themselves win. The point is that Pisker let outside things influence his performance on the field, and not letting this happen is a lesson that players need to learn early in their careers.

One year during the playoffs, we heard about a pitcher on the other club who always pitched in the same sweatshirt and was obsessed with the idea of it being good luck for him. You guessed it: we stole the sweatshirt out of the clubhouse a few hours before the game he was due to start, he was devastated when he couldn't find it, he got bombed, and we won an important playoff game. He will finally find out about this if he reads this book.

> **Tips for Future Pros**
> Nobody can play head games with you if you believe in yourself. Knowing that you have prepared properly gives you this confidence.

> **Inside Baseball**
> Notice that the hitters who wear padding and other guards on their arms stand on top of the plate in order to gain an advantage over the pitcher. The players who are the most noticeable are Barry Bonds, Mo Vaughn, and Craig Biggio.

Game Situations for a Hitter

Your job is to get on base any way you can. You should have the ability to bunt for a base hit and have good speed and baserunning ability. It is also important that you make the starter work early in the game. One of the keys in winning at the big-league level is to do whatever possible to get the starting pitcher out of the game before the end of six innings. If you accomplish this, you will be facing a team's second-line pitching. If he goes seven, you might see nothing but premium guys out of the pen the remainder of the game. Most managers and hitting coaches keep track of the pitches that the opposing starter throws each inning and take pride in how soon they can get him out of the game. The Texas Rangers are very good at teaching this concept.

Leading Off an Inning

Whether you hit in the top of the order or hit cleanup, there are times when you lead off an inning. Depending on the score, you must also work the count and try to get on base.

Tips for Future Pros
You must know the score in order to know how to react to each situation. Smart hitters always know what their job is when they get to the plate for each at-bat.

Two Outs and Nobody On

Coming to the plate with two outs and nobody on base is not a lot different from leading off an inning, but you are much more likely to swing early in the count and try to drive the ball. Also, if you have a reasonable chance to stretch a single to a double, give it a try. It is doubtful that your club will get two more hits with two outs to score you, so be bold and try to get into scoring position right away.

Inside Baseball
Watch the runners on first and see if you can tell if their leads increase when they are going to steal. Watch the signs from the third-base coach and see if you can pick up the sequences that he uses.

Hitting While the Runner Is Stealing

When the runner is stealing, your job is to protect him any way you can. If the pitcher has delivered the ball in a hurry (as in a slide step), you should try and put the ball in play or at least foul it off. If you just stand there because the ball is a little outside or high, the runner is going to be out in most cases. If the pitcher has a slow delivery to the plate and the runner gets a great jump, take the pitch, for he should be safe easily. In most cases you won't be able to tell what kind of jump the runner has, so just swing through a pitch to protect the runner (the catcher can't come out as aggressively if you swing). Hitting with a potential base stealer on first is a tough job because you find yourself hitting behind in the count much of the time.

The Hit-and-Run

When the hit-and-run is on, the hitter must swing unless the ball is in the dirt. The runners don't get great jumps on a hit-and-run, for they must make sure the ball is delivered to the plate before they break. It is your job to hit the ball somewhere on the ground. A fly ball will defeat the purpose and will at times result in a double play. Some experts will tell you that you should hit the ball through the empty hole (usually the second-base side for a right-handed hitter). Most of the time the second baseman will cover with a right-handed hitter at the plate, but there is no guarantee. This isn't rocket science, so just hit the ball anywhere on the ground. Also, after you hit the ball and it goes through the infield, the runner on first will always get to third. Be alert, and if the defense throws to third you may be able to cruise into second on the throw.

Man on Second, No Outs

In this situation, you should wait and get a pitch that you can hit to the right side of the field on the ground. If you are a right-handed hitter, wait for a fastball on the outside half and go with it (it should be easy if you have been working off the tee). For a left-handed hitter, wait for a fastball on the inside half or an off-speed pitch over the plate. You must do whatever is necessary to get your teammate to third with one out. If you choose to use a bunt for a base hit toward the second baseman, make sure you get the ball past the pitcher.

Man on Third, Infield Back, Less than Two Outs

What a dream—they are giving your team a run and you a free run batted in. All you need to do is to hit a ground ball up the middle and, presto, a free run. Wait for a good pitch to hit and don't panic. As easy as this assignment sounds, nobody is any good driving in a run if they swing at a bad pitch.

Man on Third, Infield In

Be patient and make the pitcher get the ball up. He will try to work you downstairs, for his infield is playing in and he must have a ground ball. Your job is to get a pitch up so that you can either hit it in the air deep enough to score the runner from third or get a base hit.

Man on First, Sacrifice Bunt in Order

The pitcher must throw you a strike. If he throws a couple of balls (many pitchers have trouble throwing strikes in an obvious bunting situation), the manager may change to hit-and-run, or, who knows, he may even walk you. You should bunt the ball softly toward the first baseman. He has to hold the runner on first and will be the last one in to cover his ground. Try to kill the ball (take the speed off) by pulling back with both hands at the same time and/or bunting the ball near the end of the bat or both.

Men on First and Second, Sacrifice Bunt in Order

The same fundamentals apply, but bunt the ball harder at the third baseman and make him field the ball. Watch the defense; if they run the shortstop toward third and charge the third baseman (wheel play), it opens up the infield and you may want to slug bunt (a short quick swing). See Chapter 5 for detailed bunt play defenses.

Suicide squeeze.   If you give it away too soon, they will pitch out or knock you down, and the runner will be out. Wait until the pitcher's arm starts forward, and it will be too late for him to change the flight of the ball. Obviously, you must bunt the ball (at least foul it off). If you bunt through it, the runner is out. Throw the bat at it if you have to, but you must get a piece. Bunt the ball to the middle of the field. If you and the runner execute the squeeze properly, there is no defense to stop it.

What Great Hitters Do

Using Visualization (Mark McGwire)

I coached in Oakland for years, and Mark McGwire was one of the smartest hitters I ever saw. He had a routine from the dugout to the on-deck circle to the batter's box that is incredible. He would get ready with his helmet and batting gloves and stand silently watching the pitcher from the corner of the dugout. During this period, he would visualize all of the previous successful at-bats that he had against this pitcher. As he approached the on-deck circle, he continued watching and measuring all of the pitches. He then formed a mental picture of himself hitting every kind of pitch that the pitcher had for a line drive.

By the time he stepped into the box, he had already had success (in his mind) against this pitcher. It made the entire process easier. People got the wrong impression of Mark McGwire. People thought that he was just a muscle man with 17-inch forearms. Of course he was strong, but he didn't swing hard, he just used his body efficiently. He had a terrific idea of the strike zone and rarely swung at bad pitches. He was a power hitter, but more important, he was a sound fundamental hitter with great patience and balance. He also used a relatively light bat for a guy his size.

> **Inside Baseball**
>
> Watch the runner on third in a squeeze situation. You will know if a squeeze is possible if the following factors are present:
>
> - The game is close.
> - There is a runner on third and one out.
> - There is a weak hitter at the plate (or the pitcher in the National League).
>
> For more good hitting information, see the book *Play Better Baseball*.

Just Cocky Enough (Steve Finley)

I have known Steve since the early 1990s, when I was a coach in Houston. He came to us, and we were told that he could just be a backup outfielder with a good glove and a questionable bat. He turned into one of the most productive hitters in the game of baseball while maintaining a Gold Glove in center field. Players who are All-Stars on both sides of the ball are rare.

When Steve was labeled a backup, somebody forgot to tell Steve. He worked extremely hard and had a certain cocky approach that led to him becoming a great player. He is one of the nicest guys in the majors, but when he is on the field, he just flat believes he can do anything. I feel that this has made the difference in his career. If you don't believe in yourself, who will?

Emotional Control (Jeff Bagwell)

I learned a lot watching Jeff Bagwell for three years while I was coaching in Houston. I've never seen a hitter control his emotions like this guy.

He was always the same whether he hit three home runs or struck out three times. While some players smash bat racks and destroy dugout restrooms, Jeff Bagwell sets the standard for emotional stability. This steadiness and consistency is what Jeff is all about. Forget that he has the body of a Greek god, his real strength is above the shoulders. Jeff is an all-around smart player. He is a great first baseman and a great baserunner. I began watching him during his Rookie of the Year season of 1991, and the qualities of this young man were obvious from the beginning.

Jeff has a plan for every at-bat. When the opposing pitcher is warming up (Jeff usually hits third or fourth in the order), he watches every pitch the pitcher throws. This process continues until he steps into the box to face the pitcher. He will step out and take two practice swings with his back to home plate and then assume his position in the box.

Although Jeff is basically a pull hitter, he can use the whole field as well as anybody when a pitcher pitches him away. I've seen him hit tape-measure shots to left (like the upper-deck shot in the old Three Rivers Stadium, about 550 feet) as well as huge shots to center field and right field. Jeff is at his best when the game is on the line and is one of the toughest outs in the big leagues. He is the poster boy for mental skills.

A Perfect Swing (Tony Gwynn)

Tony Gwynn was an instructor at the San Diego School of Baseball from 1982 to 1999. During that time I had many conversations with him about hitting. Even in his prime years he took more than 50,000 swings a year, more in the early days. Think about this for a minute, and compare it to your work ethic. You would have to average nearly 140 swings a day to match this total. I remember one home stand when he took extra hitting for five consecutive days in July. He was hitting .390 at the time. Sure, Tony Gwynn has God-given talent, but much of his success is because of hard work.

Tips for Future Pros

If you want to become a big leaguer, watch great hitters and notice their balance and how still their heads are during their swings.

While some lesser hitters panic and move around in the batter's box from at-bat to at-bat, Tony stayed in the same spot for his whole career.

Whether the pitcher was a hard thrower, a soft tosser with a great change-up, left-handed, or right-handed, he stayed put. This is the way you learn the strike zone. The knowledge of the strike zone coupled with his phenomenal bat control combined to make him very difficult to strike out. He also used the smallest bat in the major leagues at 33 inches and 30.5 ounces. Players who use big bats normally have small batting averages and huge strikeout numbers. At age 41 Tony was still using the batting tee on a regular basis and taking tons of extra hitting.

If You Don't Know, Ask (Alan Trammell)

Alan Trammell was a gifted athlete. He could have been a big-time college basketball player if he had chosen to. His hand-eye coordination was something to behold. As a hitter, he had more than one thousand RBI and was one of the toughest to strike out in the majors during his 20-year career with the Detroit Tigers. Even as a teenager when he first began at the San Diego School of Baseball, he was always asking questions about baseball and especially hitting. When players like Pete Rose, George Brett, and Willie Stargell were guest instructors at the school, Alan was always around them trying to pick their brains and learn from anybody and everybody. This quality helped lead to a great career and someday will make him a great big-league manager.

Another point worth mentioning is that nobody stays more focused and concentrates any better than Alan Trammell. His ability to stay "in" a game regardless of the score is what I noticed about him the most.

Don't Try to Pull the Ball (Edgar Martinez)

Hitting instructors everywhere have been teaching the "inside-out" swing for many years. Edgar Martinez has the best pure swing in baseball. Tony Gwynn, Rafael Palmeiro, and others have beautiful swings, but Edgar is simply the best at staying inside the ball, and letting the ball get to him. You could look at it as the opposite of trying to pull the ball. Edgar is a perfect example of a guy who lets the ball get deep or what used to be called "waiting on the ball." He is proof that a person doesn't have to pull the ball to have power. His head is dead still, and he is very patient at the plate. He will chase a high fastball once in a while but rarely gets himself out by chasing a bad pitch.

It is so important, I'll say it again: there is nothing wrong with pulling the ball, but there is everything wrong with trying *to pull the ball.*

The Courage to Make Adjustments (Luis Gonzalez)

I put Luis in here because of his ability to adjust. He got tired of being a singles and doubles hitter and changed his approach. Some people say he got on the weights, some say he opened his stance so that he could pull the ball more, and some say he just matured as a hitter.

There is no doubt that he is a smarter hitter today than he was a few years ago. He knows what to look for on what counts from each pitcher. I think that before he became such a smart hitter, he gave up one or two at-bats a game and got himself out by swinging at bad pitches.

He did open his stance some, and I think he now sees the ball better than ever before. This gave him the confidence that he could hit all pitches in all zones. He trusts himself and his natural ability. Luis Gonzalez now believes *that he can hit, and he had the courage to change his stance in the middle of his career.*

The Pitcher's Brain

The Mechanics

If you're pitching out of the windup, you should take a small step back (figure 4.1), place your foot in front of the rubber (figure 4.2), arrive at a balance point (figure 4.3), take an easy stride arriving at the loaded position (figure 4.4), rotate and finish with your head down toward your target (figure 4.5). From the stretch, you come set (figure 4.6) and lift your lead foot to assume the balanced point.

Simply stated, you should divide your delivery into three parts. Part one is everything you do to arrive at your balance point, part two is the easy stride to the loaded position, and part three is the rotation of the trunk and the finish. Try to take your head down as you complete the delivery. It is easy to throw the ball belt-high, but a pitcher must work hard to finish and throw the ball at the knees consistently. If you think of taking your rear shoulder all the way to the target, you will finish properly.

For a more detailed breakdown of the mechanics, see *Play Better Baseball*.

We recommend that pitchers pitch from the stretch only during their first two years. This includes high school pitchers who come into relief from the field or are part-time pitchers on their teams. This keeps the delivery much simpler and lets the pitcher throw more strikes and develop confidence.

Tips for Future Pros

Smart pitchers don't try to throw hard. The command of your fastball is more important than the velocity. A fastball sinking at the knees at 82 miles an hour is much more effective than a fastball belt-high down the middle at 95.

The Pitches Necessary for Success

You must have a fastball that you can control with movement, a breaking pitch (past the age of 11 or so), and a change-up to compete at the higher levels. When

4.1 When pitching out of the windup, take a very small step back so that you can remain on center to the target.

4.2 Next, place your foot in front of the rubber to provide for a firm base.

4.3 As you lift your free leg into the balance point, you should have your weight over your back foot.

4.4 After an easy stride, you arrive in what is called the "loaded position," ready to rotate and come forward.

4.5 Next, rotate fully and take your head down toward your target.

4.6 From the stretch position, you simply lift your leg to the balance point and follow the same mechanical routine.

you can control your fastball to the inside and outside third of the plate 75 percent of the time and have a change-up that you can throw for a strike 75 percent of the time, you have graduated from "thrower" to "pitcher." Become a "strike machine" with your fastball before you start trying to develop other pitches.

Fastball

The lone common denominator among successful pitchers is the command of their fastball. A cross-seam or four-seam fastball (same thing) is the basic grip

4.7 The basic grip for all players is the four-seam or cross-seam grip. This allows for a true flight of the ball.

4.8 A popular sinker grip used by most big leaguers is also called a two-seam grip.

4.9 This grip will either sink or sail (have some cutting action), depending on the size of the pitcher's hands.

4.10 This is an excellent grip for pitchers with small hands.

that all pitchers should start out with (figure 4.7). Three different grips for the sinker or two-seam fastball (figures 4.8, 4.9, and 4.10) are effective for different pitchers with different sized hands. One of these grips will provide you with the movement on your fastball that will be necessary to face good hitters.

The hat drill. I use a drill called the "hat drill" to help pitchers improve the command of their fastballs. Have the catcher walk up two steps in front of home plate. It is wise to use a portable plate for a target, but if you don't have one, just throw down your hat (hence the name of the drill). Working off the mound and throwing easy (about 60 percent), move the ball in and out and up and down randomly, about 30 to 40 throws to different locations. The catcher (he can be another player) can move the target from pitch to pitch and make the pitcher hit different locations.

This is the way you pitch in a game: up and down and in and out with your fastball. It is a waste of time to have the catcher sit down the middle all the time, for you will not develop the skill of hitting a target with your fastball. As you take your head to the outside corner, then the inside corner, you should visualize an imaginary line between your head and the glove. There is a direct path that your head takes to the target (the glove). The path is slightly different from location to location. I call these "lanes." As you practice throwing down these lanes, you are gaining better command of your fastball. Only through repetition will you master the control of your fastball necessary to become a professional success. Because you are throwing easy, you can do the hat drill every day, if you choose, without risk of injury.

Try doing this drill with your eyes closed. Come to the set position, look at your target, close your eyes, and hit it. You will notice that you still see a vivid picture of the glove after your eyes close. Throwing with your eyes closed will make you *feel* your mechanics and improve your overall balance.

Curveball

You can learn a relatively safe curve by gripping the ball along a long seam with your middle finger (figure 4.11), placing the thumb directly across from the middle finger (figure 4.12), and pointing your index finger at your target (figure 4.13). You then simply throw the ball. Don't twist it or try to "help" it by turning it. Keep your hand straight down the side of the ball (figure 4.14), and point the fingers out toward your target (the catcher's glove). If the ball is breaking nearly straight down, you

4.11 Attain a good curveball grip by placing the middle finger on the long seam of the ball.

4.12 Notice that the thumb is placed on the other side of the ball from the middle finger.

4.13 By pointing the index finger at the target, you will create the proper spin on your curve.

4.14 Your hand should come down the side of the ball to achieve the best break.

4.15 If your hand rotates around or under the ball, you can do serious damage to your elbow.

are throwing it correctly. If you have considerable lateral break, you are coming around it, and it will be both ineffective and dangerous. If you are twisting the ball (figure 4.15) and trying to make it break more, you can do serious damage to your elbow.

At the San Diego School of Baseball, we teach kids curveballs at age 10 or 11 if they are already throwing some form of breaking ball. Almost without exception,

Tips for Future Pros

Younger pitchers before age 15 should be limited to 20 percent curves of their total pitches, and nobody should be throwing more than 30 percent breaking balls at any level.

4.16 This is a popular grip for a cutter. This pitch will break across but will not come down much.

4.17 A slider is also gripped off-center but will come down and across when it breaks.

pitchers are usually throwing some form of a curve in an unsafe manner, and we show them the proper technique. Remember that no breaking ball is safe if the pitcher falls in love with it and is allowed to overuse it.

Inside Baseball

When you are at a professional game, watch the pitcher warm up between innings. He will motion to the catcher as to what pitch he is throwing. His glove will move straight out for fastball, down for curveball, and out and back for change-up.

Developing a sharper and shorter break. The one thing that pitchers with good curveballs have in common is a strong grip. Shake hands with Nolan Ryan, Darryl Kile, or anyone with a great curveball, and you will feel the difference. A strong grip allows you to generate faster rotation (spin) on the ball.

Using the proper mechanics will also help. If you try to "reach out" and throw your curve out toward the target and not up, you will take the hump out and have a sharper, quicker break. Because all of your pitches should have the same arm speed, you should try to throw your curve hard. A good target is the catcher's mitt.

Slider and Cutter

The slider and "cut fastball" are pitches for more advanced pitchers. The cutter is thrown with a slightly off-center grip (figure 4.16) and with no twisting or turning action at all. Because some pitchers will turn on the ball and come down the side when they are young and inexperienced, you should be careful when teaching this pitch to youth league pitchers because of the danger to the elbow. The cutter should have a short break and stay up with no downward break.

The slider is also gripped off-center and simply thrown like a fastball (figure 4.17). Because you have more surface of the ball in contact with the middle finger than you have with the cutter, the ball will break

Tips for Future Pros

If you want a future in baseball, then don't throw a slider before the age of 18.

down and across 10 to 12 inches. If the break on the ball is big one time and short the next, the pitcher is twisting or turning around the ball and the pitch will never be consistent. Remember, if you twist the ball, it is not only tough on your elbow but the break will never be the same from pitch to pitch. Former big leaguers James Rodney Richard and Larry Andersen had the best sliders of any pitchers that I ever coached.

Many pitchers, including lots of major leaguers, twist their sliders instead of letting the grip create the break. This causes an inconsistent break on your

4.18 You choke a change-up into your palm, place your thumb underneath, and then just get comfortable with your other fingers. Your grip is *your* grip.

4.19 Many young pitchers try to throw a "circle change" that they can't control. This is an advanced pitch, because it requires mature hands to control it.

slider, making it very difficult to control, and is very dangerous and causes big elbow problems in the long term. Remember that the proper way to throw a slider is to grip it off-center and throw it like a fastball. This method creates the same spin and therefore the same amount of break each time.

Change-Up

Developing a change-up is just about the best thing that you can do for your career as a pitcher. You begin learning a change by getting your own personal grip. Open up your pitching hand fully, and choke the ball back in your hand (figure 4.18). Close your hand around the ball and you have your grip. Don't copy someone else's grip. Many young kids try to throw a "circle change" (figure 4.19) that they can't control.

Grab the ball with your change grip and think, "I'm throwing a fastball with a different grip." This is the only way that you will show the hitter the arm speed of a fastball and therefore fool the best hitters. Try to throw your change right down the middle. You want swings on your change, for the change-up is a pitch that gets outs. Don't change the grip if you can't get it over at first or if it gets hit. It will take at least a year of hard work to develop a good change-up, but it will be worth it, for there is no greater weapon against good hitters.

Split-Fingered Fastball

My partner Roger Craig and I developed the "split" with the help of others at the San Diego School of Baseball during a winter of the late 1970s. Pitching instructors Roger Craig, Tom House, Brent Strom, Dave Smith, and others began experimenting with a "Little League change-up." The original name was actually the "split-fingered change." Roger Craig took it to Detroit and changed the

4.20 The split-fingered fastball becomes dangerous when a pitcher splits his fingers too far apart and locks up his wrist.

4.21 As long as the wrist remains loose and the fingers are not too far apart, the split is safe to throw.

name to "split-fingered fastball" so pitchers would think "fastball" as they threw it. He taught it to the major league pitchers, and it took off from there.

The split is not dangerous unless the pitcher splits his fingers too far apart (figure 4.20), which restricts the wrist and therefore puts pressure on the elbow. Because the pitch should be used as a change-up for young pitchers, they should grip it with the fingers just outside the seams (figure 4.21) and simply throw a fastball. If your wrist feels nice and loose like it does when you throw your fastball, then the chances are you are throwing it correctly.

> **Inside Baseball**
> Seventy percent of pitches in a major league game are on the outside half of the plate.

Using Your Pitches in Sequence

Some coaches overdo scouting reports and try to pitch to hitters' weaknesses even though they have a pitcher on the mound who has no control of his fastball. It is impossible to exploit weaknesses unless the pitcher is far enough advanced that he can throw his fastball where he wants at least 75 percent of the time. A pitcher should always stay with his strengths. If the hitter at the plate is a low-ball hitter and you are a sinkerball pitcher, throw your sinker.

Use the hitter's strength against him. If he likes the low ball, throw him low pitches just down out of the zone. If he can hit a high fastball, throw him high fastballs across the chest. Hitters will chase pitches that are just outside of their favorite zones.

When in Doubt, Stay Away

Start most hitters with fastballs away. The old saying is, "If he is going to beat me, he'll have to beat me away." Having the ability to throw your fastball low and away at any time is a huge advantage for a pitcher. Curt Schilling told me once that he feels that he can throw his four-seam fastball down and away for a strike 90 percent of the time.

Inside Baseball

Notice how some hitters will be fooled so easily with off-speed pitches like a change-up. They will jump to their front foot and lose all leverage and power. The best hitters will maintain their balance and get better swings on change-ups.

Tips for Future Pros

If you don't pitch inside, good hitters will smoke your best low and away pitches the second or third time you face them. You must command your fastball to both sides of the plate. Remember that this doesn't mean hitting people.

The most important pitch you throw is strike one. If your goal is to get the hitter out in four pitches or fewer (three or fewer for a professional pitcher), then you must be aggressive and come right after the hitter. After you get ahead with good low fastballs on the outside half, then you can use your other pitches. Going in and out with your fastball is still the best sequence of all.

Nothing upsets a hitter more than a pitcher who can throw his fastball to both sides of the plate. Remember to back your pitches up once in a while, that is, throw a fastball in, then throw a fastball in again.

You may mix in your next best control pitch on the fringes of the zone to get the hitter to chase; then you should come right back with an aggressive low fastball.

Another favorite sequence of mine is going "up the ladder": throwing a fastball letter-high and then throwing the next one a bit higher. The hitter will often chase that bad pitch, especially with two strikes. This sequence works particularly well when the hitter has an uppercut swing. Most hitters cannot hit the ball above the belt if you have an above-average fastball. In fact, some big-league hitters go through their entire careers unable to lay off this tempting but hard to hit high fastball.

To be effective, you must also pitch inside. A fastball thrown six to eight inches off the plate at the belt won't hit anyone (the hitter will move), it has a chance to "jam" the hitter, and it at least will set up pitches on the outside half of the plate, where most of your pitches will or should be thrown.

If your curve and/or your change-up has progressed to the point that you can throw them for strikes at least 60 percent of the time, then you may use them on fastball counts like 2–0, 2–1, 3–1, and 3–2. Until you can command these pitches with this proficiency, your second and third pitches are only useful when you are ahead in the count.

One of the most critical counts is 1–1; Greg Maddux calls it the most important count during an at-bat. Why? Because the next pitch needs to be a strike: a 1–2 count is *much* better than 2–1. Pitchers should try to stay away from 3–2 counts with fewer than two outs and men on because the other club may start the runners and you'll lose your double play.

Pitching Around Hitters

When a manager wants a pitcher to pitch around a hitter, he should make his intentions very clear. If he wants you to throw four wide ones with no chance of the ball being put into play, he should just intentionally walk the hitter. Lots of things can go wrong (bad pitch, wild pitch), and it makes no sense for the manager to take a chance when the game is close (which it usually is when this situation comes up). If the manager wants you to try to "nibble" the fringes of the strike zone for a couple of pitches and walk the hitter if he doesn't swing, he needs to tell you this. If he just wants you to be careful and stay away from a fastball to hit, he should lay this plan out clearly to you and the catcher.

Tips for Future Pros

Pitchers who fall short in their careers usually develop what I call "minor league habits." That is, they don't have enough command or enough courage to throw pitches other than the fastball on counts like 2–0, 2–1, 3–1, and 3–2. They are told, "Don't get beat on your third-best pitch," and I say that on these counts, your fastball just may be your third-best pitch, at least for this particular situation.

Pitching with a Base Open

Successful pitchers know when to be aggressive and when to be careful. When first base is open and the run means little, why should you give in to the hitter? There are times when big-league managers will even tell their pitchers to "pitch carefully, and I don't care if you walk him" when there are runners on first and third, or even first and second.

Pitching in a "Shutdown Inning"

After your team scores some runs and goes ahead or gets back into a game when you were way behind, you must go out and throw a zero up on the board. This "shutdown inning" will get your team back in the dugout and will give them a great lift emotionally.

Stay with What You Do Best

Please remember to rely on your strengths as a pitcher. When you try to overanalyze and pitch to the weaknesses of the hitter, it normally just gets you behind in the count and in trouble. For example, if you are told that the hitter can't hit a curve and you can't throw your curve close, how will you use this information to help you get him out? If you throw him two straight curves in the dirt, you are 2–0 and now you must throw him the one pitch that you can get over and the one pitch that he can hit, a fastball. You are much better off throwing him a fastball down in the zone on the first pitch and taking your chances.

Know Your Umpire

Umpires, like ballplayers, have definite patterns. There is one professional umpire whom everyone calls "Low Ball" because he calls the low pitch better than anyone else does. If he is umpiring the plate, you can work the bottom of the zone all night. The important thing is that he is consistent. Veteran umpire Bob Davidson was known as "Balking Bob" and would call a balk on anything close to a balk. Bob was a great umpire, but when he was working the game, you had to watch yourself executing pickoff moves. I think that he was just trying to get it right. All-Star Curt Schilling keeps a book on every umpire and the tendencies that they have. This information helps him win and is part of being a smart pitcher. Most good pitchers, catchers, and pitching coaches discuss the umpire working the plate each night before the game.

Pregame Routines

A big-league starting pitcher arrives at the ballpark about two and a half hours before game time. National League pitchers who have to hit will get dressed early and go out to hit in batting practice. American League starters get partially dressed and attend a pitchers and catchers meeting after batting practice. After the meeting, the pitcher will get a stretch or rubdown by the trainer before get-

Inside Baseball

Watch where the catcher sets up for the pitch and how close the pitcher comes to hitting the target. Experienced pitchers and big winners will amaze you with how often they nail their target.

ting dressed and heading down to warm up for the game. Some star players even have personal trainers who help them prepare between starts.

A Day in the Life of a Starting Pitcher

10:00 A.M.	Get up and eat a good breakfast.
11:00 A.M.–2:00 P.M.	Relax, watch television, read, etc.
2:00 P.M.	Have lunch; carbohydrates are a popular item. No big steaks, etc.
2:45 P.M.	Leave for the ballpark.
3:30 P.M.	Get partially dressed, watch TV, hang around the clubhouse. National League pitchers go out and bunt and hit during batting practice.
5:30 P.M.	Look at tapes of opposing team and/or attend pitchers' and catchers' meeting with pitching coach and/or manager.
6:00 P.M.	Get a rubdown and/or stretch by the trainers.
6:20 P.M.	Put on uniform and go down to warm up.
6:40 P.M.	Run sprints and continue to stretch lower body.
6:45 P.M.	Begin throwing in bullpen.
7:00 P.M.	Finish warm-ups and head for dugout.
7:05 P.M.	Game time.

Warming Up

Most starting pitchers make between 45 and 60 pitches while warming up for their starts. I really believe lots of pitchers throw way too many warm-ups before a game. I've seen some throw for 20 minutes hard and make 80 to 90 pitches. Pitchers should begin their warm-ups with fastballs away (right-handed pitchers begin with pitches on the first-base side of plate). To get the ball to the far side of the plate, a pitcher must finish his delivery properly. This creates good habits and a basis for a good fundamental delivery. Some pitchers like to play catch for a couple of minutes then "long toss" (120–140 feet) before they begin their warm-ups. There are a hundred different routines; each pitcher should develop one that works for him.

Of the pitchers I've coached, Cy Young Award–winner Doug Drabek had the best routine. He would throw a few balls short of the mound (about 54 feet), a few behind the mound (about 70 feet), then step up and throw exactly 42 pitches. No, he didn't count them, I did (I counted all my pitchers' warm-ups). He was very disciplined, and he had a solid routine that worked for him. He would throw 18 or 19 fastballs, 10 to 12 curveballs, 4 to 6 change-ups, and finish with fastballs in and out. I wouldn't tell him when to quit or tell him the total; he just knew, 42 every time. Well, OK, sometimes 44, but never any more. We would talk casually during the first 20 pitches or so, but at the halfway mark I would shut up and let him concentrate. I believe that Drabek, Curt Schilling, and Kenny Rogers were the most focused of all the pitchers I ever worked with.

Tips for Future Pros

It is usually not a good idea to go in with a 2–1 or 3–1 count because the umpire won't call it, and the hitter won't swing because he is looking for a pitch to drive out over the plate. Going in with two strikes is a great idea because the hitter is now protecting the plate and will most likely swing at the ball on the inside corner. You can "freeze" the hitter on this count because he will probably be looking out over the plate.

Inside Baseball

Notice how the best hitters adjust from pitch to pitch depending on how the pitcher uses his sequences.

The Rotation

A pitcher who pitches on a Monday (day one) will rest and stretch on Tuesday (day two), throw on the side on Wednesday (day three) for about 15 minutes, rest

Thursday (day four) and Friday (day five), and pitch again on Saturday (day one). Some pitching coaches (I was one) encourage their pitchers to throw off the mound twice, on days three and four. I feel that getting on the mound twice between starts is very productive and leads to the ability to "repeat" (be consistent) with your delivery. Leo Mazzone of the Atlanta Braves, who has coached future Hall of Famers Greg Maddux and Tom Glavine, agrees and has used this practice for years with much success. I believe that many big-league pitching coaches are now having pitchers throw twice between starts. I have always felt that pitchers don't throw enough off the mound in order to develop the consistency that they could.

> **Tips for Future Pros**
>
> Develop your own routine. You may use some of the ideas here to help, but be yourself and develop your own plan. There is never a reason to throw more than 60 pitches in the bullpen.

Relief Pitchers

Pitchers nearly always know their roles and are prepared when the call comes for them to warm up. If they are smart, they have watched the game and know who is coming up and what they have done so far in the game. A good bullpen coach will keep a dialogue going about the game, ask questions, and keep everyone thinking baseball. Unfortunately, some clubs have coaches who just carry the ball bag down to the bullpen before the game and back when it's over. The best bullpen coaches help you win lots of games. To me, the bullpen coach is like an assistant pitching coach; Glen "EZ" Ezell is the best I've seen.

Because most pro teams play every day for more than six months, relief pitchers are used quite a bit. Playing time will usually go in streaks, with several appearances one week, then a week off. Of course, the better you are and the more you get the job done, the more you will pitch with the game on the line. The closer must be ready every night if possible. More and more pitchers have defined roles even in college baseball and in the low minors.

> **Inside Baseball**
>
> Go down by the bullpen and watch the starting pitcher warm up. Notice his routine, and see how it varies from the next pitcher you watch. Every pitcher has his own program.

They call it "Trevor time" in San Diego when AC/DC's "Hells Bells" plays on the public-address system and Padres closer Trevor Hoffman enters the game. His pregame routine is one of my favorites. He comes to the ballpark very early and runs his butt off; I believe few relief pitchers in the game have been in the physical shape that Trevor is in. After running, he goes in, takes a shower, and gets dressed. He comes out and bunts and hits with the other pitchers, then he does his shagging in the outfield while the position players hit. After batting practice, he grabs a bite to eat, attends meetings, talks with the press, and just hangs out. When the game starts, he goes down to the bullpen and watches the game for the first four or five innings. He watches the hitters, talks baseball with the other relievers, and relaxes. In the fifth inning, he goes back to the clubhouse and showers again, gets dressed, and listens to the game. In the seventh, he returns to the bullpen to get mentally and physically ready.

> **Inside Baseball**
> Go down by the bullpen and watch a reliever warm up. You will see how he does things differently from how the starters do them. He will watch the game situation and time his warm-up so that he peaks just as he is called into the game. Certain relief pitchers have certain roles and pitch at specific times in the game, ahead or behind, or are situational guys who might face hitters only in specific situations. An example is a left-handed reliever who is used specifically to get a left-handed hitter out.

When it's time for Trevor to warm up, he throws several balls from behind the mound and then goes up to the mound and throws about 20 to 25 pitches. He gets all of his pitches (including what I think is the best change-up in all of baseball) ready and enters the game. Like most experienced relievers, he stops when he is ready and watches the game. Inexperienced pitchers have a tendency to throw too much and leave their best stuff in the bullpen. He is also very disciplined, with 25 pitches and five showers (counting the one in the morning and the one after the game). One of the best closers in baseball history is also one of the hardest working and surely the cleanest.

Babying Prospects

Pitchers now are overprotected by every organization in baseball. They are on strict pitch counts and never throw without proper rest between starts. Relievers are never allowed to throw three days in a row, and managers are careful with back-to-back days even when they have pitched just one inning. With all the money involved now, ball clubs won't take any chances with their pitchers. Agents complain, threaten, and usually get their way when their clients are being used either too much or not enough in their opinions. Some of this protection is good and necessary, but much of it can be counterproductive; for example, a pitcher who has too many restrictions on pitch counts will not get the valuable experience of learning how to pitch out of jams by extending himself.

How Much Should You Throw?

I know it sounds like a contradiction when I say kids don't throw enough and kids shouldn't be allowed to throw too much. Remember that kids can throw *easy* every day and in fact need to throw more often when working on their accuracy. Second, it is maximum-effort game pitches that take their toll on a young arm—specifically the elbow and the shoulder when the joints are still growing. Overtraining is a problem throughout youth sports. Parents and coaches can push kids to the point where they hate the sport. Kids need to play with no structure and no

> **Inside Baseball**
>
> A major leaguer on the disabled list not only gets full salary but full credit for days on the pension, and so on. I have known players who have missed two consecutive years and then were eligible for arbitration because the time counted the same as if they were playing.

supervision at times. They absolutely don't need a coach or parent looking over their shoulders pushing them every day. Not only do they need physical rest, but they need to get away from sports emotionally and just play and have fun with their friends.

Coaches Don't Always Know Best

College

The majority of college coaches are good baseball men; the only real abuse at the highest levels is coming from a handful of selfish coaches. Coaches who overpitch their best guys simply don't care about the future of these players. I had one pitcher with me in Houston who told me that he had once thrown 270 pitches in a college game. I have worked with at least 10 other pitchers with exceptional talent who entered pro ball with the damage already done. Their coaches robbed these kids of their pro careers before they began. Sure, something should be done, but sadly the NCAA has always ignored the problem. Coaches who sink to this level try to justify this behavior as "trying to win for the team." Some even say that they asked the pitcher if he was OK. How ridiculous! What 19-year-old kid is going to say he's tired or hurting when asked in front of his teammates in the middle of a regional tournament?

High School

In spite of the fact that most high school coaches do their best to learn all they can about fundamental baseball ideas, I can't tell you the times I've seen abuse at the high school level by uninformed coaches over the years. I have tried through free clinics, several books, and a million conversations to make a difference as far as protecting young arms. I thought attitudes were changing until the summer of 2001 when I ran across a few more cases of abuse in doing additional research for this book. I really don't think coaches think that they are putting their pitchers at risk; I think instead they just don't know any better.

> **Tips for Future Pros**
> Sure, you need to protect your arm by not throwing too many pitches in any one day, but basically you won't hurt your arm if you prepare, if your arm is in shape, and if you use common sense.

For example, I was in Salt Lake City in May of 2001 and read in the paper of a local high school pitcher who pitched both ends of a doubleheader in the state playoffs. Two complete games—I would estimate 150 to 200 pitches with an hour and a half break between games. The 90-minute break bothers me as much as the number of pitches. To make it worse, the pitcher had been out for a month with another injury and hadn't pitched during that period.

The Medical People

Team doctors and trainers are doing a better job than ever before in pro baseball. Even at the high school and college levels, players are treated and prepared in a safe, professional manner in most cases. Every minor league team has a licensed trainer with them at all times. Most high schools and all colleges also have professional people in charge of their athletes.

Developing Your Arm

All pitchers should be watched closely as far as their overall usage in games. The truth is that most kids either don't throw enough or they throw way too much. Kids with great talent are usually overpitched, while at least 75 percent of the players I've seen don't throw enough to ever develop a good arm, much less accuracy.

The biggest change in players that I've seen at the San Diego School of Baseball (more than 10,000 since 1971) is the increasing lack of arm strength and accuracy. There are still a few kids with terrific arm strength, but accuracy (control) has made a steady decline in all age groups and skill levels. The reason for this is really very simple.

As I mentioned earler, when my generation wanted to hit, we had to throw to each other. We were the last generation without pitching machines and batting ranges. A practice would go something like this: Jimmy Nettles, Dennis Maley, and I would go down to a park to hit (it seems like there were more fields then). Most of the time, we owned only one ball among us. Jimmy would throw to me, I would hit it out by the fence, Dennis would pick it up and throw it all the way in the air to Jimmy, and he would throw it again. We would hit 20 or 25 and rotate. Everyone pitched, hit, and fielded. We'd go around four times in about two hours. We all threw a hundred pitches at a target and threw another hundred from the fence to the mound and developed our arms. We all had better arm strength and much better accuracy. At practices now nobody throws long, and only two or three kids on a team are allowed to pitch. Pitching develops your accuracy. Batting ranges are great and very necessary in order for hitters to develop, but they shouldn't provide the only practicing you do.

Throwing Long

If you want to develop a stronger arm, you must throw using a specific drill. Throwing long (at least twice and up to three times the distance between the bases) will develop your arm strength. With a partner, three times a week, warm up at ever-increasing distances until you reach your target (120 feet or so for a Little Leaguer and up to 200 feet for a high school player). Make 20 (maximum) throws at this distance during the first three workouts making the ball bounce once to your partner. Cool down making seven or eight throws as you close the distance back down. Increase the number of maximum throws by two during each workout. The drill takes 15 to 20 minutes. Within a month, your arm will improve 20 to 30 percent. In a year, everyone you play with will notice your increased arm strength. Occasionally a player who does this drill doubles his arm strength. If you are not serious about this and don't do it according to the schedule (for example, only once a week), all you will do is make your arm sore. Unlike most promises, this drill *will* work for everyone.

Becoming More Accurate

If you want to be more accurate, there are very easy programs for you. Throw everything—baseballs, tennis balls, you name it—at a target every chance you get. Put a target on your garage and throw a ball at it for 15 minutes a day. Throw easy for 10 minutes a day to a catcher. Play catch with a friend daily for 10 minutes, making sure you hit a target (his glove, his chest, anything). Don't just get sweaty; throw at something; have a purpose. I watch kids play catch at our schools, and it makes me sick. I can tell that they never practice their throwing. If you want to be different, work at it.

Do You Work Hard Enough?

I was around a shortstop in Oakland named Mike Bordick who was as accurate a thrower as I have ever seen. How did he do it? He worked his tail off. I watched him take ground balls, and many times I would play first during practice and catch his throws. He would throw nine and ten balls in a row that would be right at the center of my chest. That kind of accuracy isn't something you're born with.

> **Tips for Future Pros**
>
> Work hard on your throwing—there simply is no other way. If you are already good, keep working; there is no such thing as being "accurate enough."

One of my partners in the San Diego School of Baseball, Alan Trammell, had one of the most accurate arms in baseball history. He grew up throwing as much as I did and was a world-class athlete to boot. He finished his 20-year career with the Tigers with a better fielding percentage than any shortstop in the Hall of Fame. Arm strength and accuracy are products of genetics (athletic ability) and hard work doing the right things (like the drills in this book).

Pitch Counts: What Is the Right Amount?

When a kid starts pitching in youth baseball, he is governed by antiquated rules that count the number of innings pitched instead of the number of pitches thrown.

There is substantial evidence that a great number of pitches in one day for pitchers 25 years of age and younger can do great damage to the shoulder and elbow or both. Another issue is the rest a pitcher receives between games. Throwing easy or less than game speed has a training effect but does little damage. Therefore, a pitcher can throw easy every day without harm, but it is the maximum-effort game tosses that have the potential for doing long-term damage.

Men Who Pitch for a Living

Major league pitchers normally throw 120 to 125 pitches in a nine-inning game. They get a full five days' rest between games. That amounts to more than a hundred hours of rest and recovery for a grown man. Some 10- or 11-year-old kids throw four innings and average 25 pitches (or more) per inning. Of course, nobody is counting, and they end up with 100 pitches or more. They are then allowed under the rules in some leagues to pitch two more innings a couple of days later. The better they are, the more they are pitched.

> **Inside Baseball**
>
> If you are interested in pitches, count the pitches at the next game that you attend. At many big-league stadiums, they make note of the pitch counts on the scoreboard. Try to see if you can notice when the starter gets tired. Most pitchers get tired at about 100 pitches or so, depending on the weather.

Travel or Select Baseball Teams

A problem in some parts of the country is the fact that some players play on more than one team. I talk to kids all the time who pitch four or five innings for one team on Saturday and four or five more on Sunday for the other team. Half the time the coaches don't even know each other or, in their defense, they don't know that this is going on. Nobody should count on the kid to volunteer the information, for he feels great and wants to pitch. There are at present no rules to prevent this from happening. Kids are having surgeries at age 11 and 12. Even if a kid survives this mismanaged system and makes it to pitching in high school, the chances are that he has already done long-term damage. This damage probably won't show up until he is on the verge of a college scholarship or a pro contract many

> **Tips for Future Pros**
>
> Never let a coach jeopardize your future by pitching you without proper rest. If you throw 100 pitches, you need four days off (divide your total pitches by 25 and take that many days off).

years later. The last line of defense to protect the kids is a parent. Just say no to overuse.

We have come up with some commonsense guidelines to protect parents and kids from arm injuries. Go to games, count pitches, and use these simple rules:

1. Make sure the pitcher arrives early enough to warm up properly before pitching. Even kids need a full 10 to 12 minutes of throwing to be ready to pitch—somewhere between 40 and 60 pitches to warm up.

2. If he comes in as a reliever, he should get 15 or 20 throws, not just 8 or whatever the rules say. You can't come in from first base and make 8 throws and be ready.

3. Multiply a pitcher's age by six, and you have a good place to cut a kid off. A 10-year-old's limit is 60 game pitches; a 14-year-old's is 84; the limit for everyone is 100. Pitchers should not throw more game pitches (maximum-effort throws) than this in any one game. Don't count the warm-ups or pitches between innings, just the game throws.

4. Rest should be calculated as follows: divide the number of pitches by 25 and give the pitcher a full day's rest for every multiple of 25. This works for any age; for example: A 12-year-old throws 75 pitches on Tuesday; he can pitch again after three days' rest, on Saturday. A 9-year-old throws 50 pitches on Thursday, he can pitch again after two days' rest, on Sunday.

5. If the pitcher feels any discomfort at all, add two days of rest; if it is still there, take him to see a sports doctor.

6. Pitchers should not pitch year-round. Give him at least two months off twice during the year.

When in Doubt, Be Conservative

Sure this is an unpopular, conservative stance, but if you care about the future of your kids in baseball, it's a no-brainer. Listen to me. I'm an expert. I have heard so many horror stories, and I'm very sensitive to this kind of abuse. Parents are too many times uninformed, coaches want to win too badly, and kids think that their arms are indestructible. This adds up to some kid somewhere being cheated out of a major league career or, at the very least, robbed of the fun of pitching in high school or college.

Remember that the damage doesn't show up for a decade in some cases. When the pitcher reaches his pitch limit, he will be throwing great, his arm will feel good, he will tell you (beg you) to let him stay in, and somebody else will have to make the call. It will take a coach with real courage to take a guy out with a shutout going in the finals. Nobody will understand the move. The coach will have to face the other players and the parents; the pitcher himself will not like it. It is then that the motives of the coach will become clear to all.

Tough Decisions

In 1991, Darryl Kile's first year in the majors, I took him out of a game in the Astrodome with a no-hitter going after six innings because of a pitch limit. I assured him that night that he would pitch a no-hitter before he was done. He didn't understand then; I'm not sure he does now. The press roasted me for the move, and the owner called me an idiot. But it was the right thing to do, and I would do it again tomorrow. On September 17, 1993, Darryl threw a no-hitter against the Dodgers. I was fired as pitching coach of the Houston Astros two weeks later. He has been an All-Star and will make more than 50 million dollars pitching.

Pitching in Games

If you've done your homework, you know the tendencies of the hitters you will face. Meet with your catcher and pitching coach, and come up with your game plan. You should meet about one and a half hours prior to game time to go over each hitter and possible pinch hitters. The pitching coach will then meet with the coach responsible for setting the defense and will place the infield and outfield in position to best defend against each hitter based on how you plan to pitch them.

Never forget that you are a fastball pitcher, that is, everything that you do as a pitcher is based on your ability to control your fastball. Even if your curve or your change-up is your best pitch, even if you don't throw real hard, everything is set up and is sequenced off your fastball.

Adjustments

As the game progresses, do whatever it takes to beat the other club. You will have to make adjustments to the game plan with several guys. I don't think you will ever pitch a game when everything goes according to plan. Your ability to adjust will become one of your greatest assets as a pitcher. Keep a positive attitude, and remember that your body language means a lot.

Don't Pace Yourself

If you are a starting pitcher, give it all you've got for as long as you can. It is a really bad idea to pace yourself so you can go deeper into the game. In fact, it is important that you come out and have a good first inning. You set the tone for the game, and as you go through the lineup the first time, you will be setting them up for each time that you face them. Use all of your pitches early to establish the fact that you can throw them all for strikes. Make sure you pitch in with your fastball the first time through the order, not just if you get in trouble. The more that you give some hitters to think about, the better off you are.

Tips for Future Pros

Put yourself in the hitter's shoes. What is his job right now?

If you come in relief, you must know the hitter that you will be facing before you leave the bullpen. You should have a plan for the first hitter long before he steps into the box. Unless he is a pinch hitter, you have probably seen him hit during the game (unless you haven't been paying attention) and have a feel for what he's doing at the plate. If he has a weakness, exploit it, or when in doubt, go with your strength. The first hitter you face is the most important (that's why the manager is bringing you in), and if you lose him, you may have failed as a reliever.

Game Situations for a Pitcher

First Hitter of the Inning

The hitter is trying to get on base, and you must get him out. Statistics show that leadoff hitters who get on base score more than half the time. Not that you should bear down more on the leadoff hitter than anyone else, but it is very important for you to get ahead with strike one and try to make him and most other hitters put the ball in play with three pitches or less.

Two Outs and Nobody on Base or Pitching with a Big Lead

This is much like the first hitter of the inning in many ways. Get ahead and make him hit the ball. Unless he hits the ball out of the ballpark, he can't hurt you, so go after him. If he doesn't have power, throw the ball down the middle and low, and see what he can do.

Pitching in a Stealing Situation

One of your biggest responsibilities is to hold runners close. This is not only about preventing steals; it is also about getting more double plays, keeping runners from going for an extra base, and keeping runners out of scoring position.

A pitcher's unloading time has much to do with how successfully he will hold runners on base. The time from when a pitcher moves a muscle and unloads the ball to when the catcher receives it should be about 1.3 seconds or less.

> **Inside Baseball**
>
> Notice how an accomplished pitcher pitches the hitters differently each time through the lineup. Good pitchers change patterns and make adjustments during the entire game depending on which pitches are working and how the hitters react to them.

When the pitcher has an unloading time slower than 1.3 seconds, something must be done. Pitchers developed the "slide step" during the 1990s. I don't like the name much because it describes the move as picking up the front foot and sliding it forward. This disrupts the natural timing of the arm swing and release point and almost always produces bad location of the pitch. Not only will you increase the chances of giving up the long ball, but it may take you several pitches to get that timing back. I think that it does more harm than good. Ideally, an organization should develop its right-handed pitchers' deliveries to be 1.3 seconds and under at all times with their normal deliveries.

If you are a pitcher, try to decrease your unloading time by one-tenth of a second each year. Before you know it, you will be down around 1.2 seconds, which will be very acceptable.

Man on Second, No Outs

If the game is close, the hitter's job is to hit a grounder to the right side and get the runner over to third. There are many more ways to score from third than from second with only one out. He should be waiting for a pitch on the first-base side of the plate. If the hitter is right-handed, you should start him with a fastball to the inside part of the plate or with an off-speed pitch for a strike. If he is left-handed, keep the ball away from him early in the count. Once you get to two strikes, the hitter's thoughts will cease to be on getting the runner over, so forget that there is a man on second and go after the hitter.

Man on Third, Infield Playing Back

We are giving up a run. Just go after the hitter as if nobody is on base. Pay no attention whatsoever to the runner on third.

Man on Third, Infield Playing In

First of all, you should pitch from a stretch. Check the runner twice, once before you begin your stretch sequence and again after you come set. The hitter will be trying to get the ball in the air, so he is looking for something up. Your job is to keep the ball on the ground. If you have a sinker, use it; if not, just keep the ball down on all of your pitches. Work the bottom of the zone and maybe he will chase something down. It is dangerous to go up the ladder (pitch up out of the zone) in this situation.

Man on First, Sacrifice Bunt in Order

Check the section on overall bunt defense in Chapter 5. Keep in mind that you must throw strikes here. If you walk the hitter, they won't have to sacrifice an out to your club. If you get behind the hitter, the offense may change to a hit-and-run to move the runner. Throw strikes, let them bunt, field your position, and let them give up the out.

Man on First and Second, Sacrifice Bunt in Order

Study the section on overall bunt defense in Chapter 5. Make sure you know the plays. Why should the defense suffer because you don't know how the play breaks down? Because you are the key to everything that happens on defense, take responsibility and make the bunt plays work effectively.

A good pitcher knows not only his job but everyone's responsibilities on bunt defense.

Inside Baseball

Watch as the shortstop fakes the runner back at second. The pitcher will deliver the ball and cover the third-base line.

Possible Squeeze Situation

Check out the section on overall defense in Chapter 5. If the offense does everything correctly, there is nothing you and your defensive club can do to prevent the squeeze. Just be ready if the runner leaves early or the hitter tips it off. If they do tip the squeeze, throw whatever pitch is called away into the batter's box. Make sure you pitch out of the stretch with a runner on third and one out in a close game.

For more good pitching information, see the book *Play Better Baseball*.

Profiles of Smart Pitchers

Pitching with Your Brain (Greg Maddux)

Maddux sets the standard for using what you have. He has a slightly below-average fastball (86 to 88 mph) but has terrific command of it. He uses both sides of the plate, makes it move, and pitches inside. There is also a 91-mph four-seamer waiting in the wings when he decides to call on it.

His curveball is sharp, and he keeps it down as well as anybody. He has a change-up that is simply one of the best. He shows the hitter the arm speed of a fastball, and it comes in at 77 or 78 mph and sinks. He uses his fastball as well as anybody except Curt Schilling.

Greg also has a mean streak. He has always shown the ability to back hitters off the plate when necessary. He uses the fastball inside to set up his other pitches better than anyone else that I have seen in years, with the exception of Pedro Martinez. He is very competitive on the mound and rarely misses a start.

People always go up to the plate to swing off Maddux because he is always around the plate. This guy never beats himself. He almost never walks a hitter, is a superb fielder, and can hit, and run the bases.

"You Will Not Beat Me" (Curt Schilling)

When you think of Curt Schilling, you think of his fastball and his strike-out totals, but he is so much more. He is not only the most determined pitcher that I ever coached, he may be one of the smartest. Doug Drabek and Kenny Rogers were very sharp, and I've coached many intelligent pitchers, but Schilling just flat-out believes in himself and knows what he wants. He never gives in. Call it guts, determination, or whatever, but he simply refuses to lose.

He also uses his fastball as well as any pitcher in the majors. He doesn't always have the 95-mph burners, but he almost always controls whatever fastball he has that day. He once told me that he feels that he can throw a fastball low and to the outside one-third of the plate anytime he wants to. What a great asset for a pitcher, for many times that is the only place that you can go for a strike when you need one.

Curt has a great slider, a new slow curve, and a devastating split that he developed in Houston before moving on to the Phillies in 1993 and becoming an All-Star.

Turning the Page (Dave Smith)

Talk about mental skills. Dave Smith was a great closer. Dave had great stuff in his first few years during the early 1980s. He had a 92-mph fast-ball that sank and ran all over the place, an outstanding curve, and a split (which he used for a change-up), and he had great control of all of them. Elbow injuries began to take their toll, and in the late 1980s and early 1990s he began losing his fastball and some of the sharpness on his curve.

He made up for any loss of stuff with strong mental skills. When "Smitty" came into a game, he took charge. He had the ability to throw his curve and split over on any count to any hitter in any situation. Lots of pitchers have only a fastball to rely on when things get tough.

Dave had the uncanny ability to turn the page and blow off any negative feelings from the day before. He had such a bright outlook each day at the ballpark and lived for the save situations that earned him two All-Star appearances and 216 lifetime saves with the Houston Astros and the Chicago Cubs. I was so happy when Dave decided to go into coaching. Qualities like these must be passed on to the next generation of players. Do I sound proud? I am; I signed Dave to his first contract out of San Diego State University.

Great Stuff and Pitching In (Pedro Martinez)

Pedro is in a class by himself. Nobody else has four pitches that are all outstanding with great command of all of them. He is also very competitive and will battle anyone for as long as it takes to beat you. He uses his pitches in great sequences and sets up his pitches as good as anyone. In many ways, he is a throwback to another era when pitchers were very aggressive.

His fastball is out of this world at 96 to 97 mph and moving like crazy. He also sinks the ball at about 90 when he cares to. His curve is very sharp and breaks very late (because of the tight spin). He has a cutter he uses effectively and a change-up that may be the best in the American League.

No pitcher in baseball pitches in like Pedro. The old-timers will tell you that this is how baseball used to be played.

Outwork the Rest (Trevor Hoffman)

Trevor began losing velocity in the late 1990s. His fastball has gone from 92 or 93 mph to about 88, but his pitching ability has increased proportionately. He has fooled around with different breaking pitches and at times shows a curve, a slider, and a cutter.

Hoffman is a very dedicated big-league player who earns every dollar he makes. There is not a wasted minute in his professional day. "I never get on a hill just to throw," he has said. Even in practice he will "never take anything for granted—getting loose, throwing in the bullpen, I always bear down."

I think he might be in better physical shape than any pitcher in the majors. He runs very hard all year round and takes care of his body in a conscientious way with a good diet and rest.

When you think of Trevor, you think of his change-up, which I think is the best in the game of baseball. His change is about 75 or so, which is nearly 15 mph slower than his fastball. A difference of 10 mph is about average, and to show the arm speed of a fastball to the hitter and give him a pitch 13 or 15 mph slower is just unbelievable. Like fellow closer and mentor Dave Smith, he has the ability to throw his change-up over the plate (or close enough to get a swing) at anytime in the count. Of course, with a great change-up to look for, the hitters are overmatched with his 88- to 90-mph fastball.

The Attitude (Dave Stewart)

Dave Stewart never had a dominating breaking ball. He pitched with a great fastball, a terrific split, and a lot of courage. He didn't make it big until he was 28 years old. He listened to pitching guru Dave Duncan and won 20 games for four years in a row for the Oakland A's. Stewart was and is a very competitive person whom you could not discourage. If you scored four runs off him in the first inning, he would find a way to beat you 5–4. My favorite story about Dave is one that I'm not even sure is true. The story goes that Roger Clemens beat him the first time they met in a particularly tough game and that afterward "Stew" said, "That man will never beat me again." They battled for years in the American League, and Clemens never did beat him again—ever.

Think Defense

Make Defense a Priority

Some coaches simply don't think that defense is that important. Practices become hitting sessions with one of two scenarios. A few coaches take the entire team to the batting range and this *is* the practice. Other coaches hold a practice at their field and 12 kids stand around while a coach throws batting practice (with one in four pitches a strike).

This process continues through high school in some cases, and it is not until a player reaches a good college program that he is exposed to the fundamentals of defense. Some minor league managers think that they are hired just to develop hitters and pitchers. When they don't teach defense like they should, the players and baseball in general are cheated out of potential complete players. The big leagues are full of players who take their defense lightly and never become the defensive players that they could be. Defensive skills and the work associated with developing them must be shoved down the throats of most players. I can never understand this thinking, for working on defense is fun and is translated into wins at every level.

> **Tips for Future Pros**
>
> Do you take your defense seriously? If your defense and/or arm accuracy is shaky, then you won't be able to play in college or pro baseball.

A Strong Defensive Beginning

It usually begins in T-ball when the basic game concepts are taught. When the ball is hit, everyone goes for the ball. An adult will yell, "Second base," and everyone on the field will try to cover second base. The first step in teaching kids to play is to divide up the responsibilities. For instance, better players shouldn't be allowed to go get everything just because they can. If a player like this continues to hog everything, he doesn't learn how to play, and neither does anyone else. I see this in youth team sports all the time.

Coaches who are obsessed with winning championships with nine- or ten-year-olds will even encourage this type of behavior. I think that kids learn faster when they are encouraged to work as a team. They must learn to divide up the responsibilities on the field and learn how to play team defense. In our schools, we move players to a different position every inning, and everyone not only has more fun but also learns the team concept of baseball.

Players should be told that there are only four possible jobs to do on defense:

- Go get the ball if it is in your area.
- Cover a base.
- Become a cutoff man.
- Back somebody up.

Even kids at ages six to eight can understand these concepts once the concepts are explained and they are allowed to play without adult commands while the play is in progress. I like to say, "There is no job called 'stand and watch'; the coach has that job." When it is explained up front to kids that they will be the ones making decisions during the game, they will really pay attention and accept that responsibility. When they are told that they will have to be aware and understand game situations (number of outs, position of baserunners, etc.), they will learn very quickly and will get "into" the game. When adults make all the decisions, why should they learn? They don't have to.

Inside Baseball

Watch how the defense adjusts from hitter to hitter during the game. Notice how other factors like who is pitching and the score determine things like the depth of the outfielders.

Positioning

If you pay attention as a defensive player, proper positioning becomes obvious. You should always begin at the straightaway position and adjust from there. To make it simple, just play half the distance between you and the player playing next to you. If you are playing the corners in the infield or the outfield, treat the foul lines as another player. If the opposing player shows you over several at-bats that he pulls the ball a great majority of the time, then play two steps to the pull field. If there is no definite pattern, just play everyone straightaway, or what is called by pros "straight up." Lots of college coaches and others pay way too much attention to positioning and overshift their players all over with every new hitter. It's not all that difficult a process, if you use common sense.

Watching the Signs for a Better Jump

Coaches and defensive players should pay attention to who is pitching and the count on the hitter. If you are a shortstop or second baseman, you will be able to see the signs from the catcher and get an edge on what pitch is coming. If you see that an off-speed pitch is called, you should lean toward the pull field as the ball crosses the hitting area. If you move or even lean too soon, you may give away the pitches. A smart coach will pick up on this and tip off his hitters; they will watch the infielder and know what pitch is coming.

> **Tips for Future Pros**
>
> If you are an outfielder, you must hit the cutoff man. When you overthrow him, every runner moves up one base and hurts the defense considerably.

When the count is 2–0 or 3–1, the outfielders should take a couple of steps back. This is an offensive count, and the hitter is more likely to drive the ball with more authority. With two strikes, you may want to take a step or two toward the off field and come in a bit. The hitter is protecting the plate and is less likely to hit for power.

Fielding Mechanics

Former major league manager Dave Garcia (Indians and Angels) once told me that players field with their feet. If you watch the best defensive players in the majors, you will see how true this really is. Roberto Alomar, Pudge Rodriguez,

Steve Finley, Greg Maddux, Kenny Rogers, and all of the Gold Glove winners have three things in common: quick feet, good hands, and a terrific work ethic.

A Breakdown of Fielding Mechanics: Keep It Simple

I divide the mechanics of fielding into five steps:

The initial setup. To assume position one, or what I call the "thinking position" (figure 5.1), stand with your feet slightly wider than shoulder width with your hands comfortably on your knees. In this position, you should be thinking about the game situation, the number of outs, and the position of the baserunners. You should be rehearsing or planning the upcoming play. Ask yourself the questions, "What will I do if a ground ball is hit to me?" or "If I catch a fly ball, what will I do?"

5.1 This is the initial position, or what I call the "thinking position." You should be rehearsing the play between pitches.

5.2 When the pitcher's arm comes forward, you switch into the "ready position."

The ready position. When the pitcher's arm comes forward, you take your hands off your knees and roll up on the balls of your feet to position two or the "ready position" (figure 5.2). Some instructors prefer that their players make a small movement up and down that basically puts the body in motion and provides for a better jump on the ball for some players. Most great defensive players have some movement as the pitch crosses the hitting area. Roberto Alomar is a great example of an infielder who moves with the pitch.

The fielding position. A good fielder should try to center every ground ball that he can (figure 5.3). You should make sure that your glove is completely open when fielding. I know that this sounds funny, but I see players field balls with partial gloves all the time (figure 5.4). It takes an effort to open the glove fully. When you field a grounder, expect the ball to stay down and work from

5.3 When you field a grounder, make sure you center the ball and turn your glove so that it is completely open to the ball.

5.4 Many infielders try to field with a "half-glove" and make a lot of errors because of it. Coaches should check their players. You may be surprised to find out how many have this basic flaw.

the ground up to field it. This will save you when the ball hits and skips instead of taking the normal hop it should take.

The close, or throwing preparation.   Before you can throw effectively, you must close off your body—that is, line up your body toward the target (figure 5.5). One action that helps is simply pulling both hands to your back shoulder after you field the ball. If the ball was fielded with a forehand (especially if you have to extend to get it) (figure 5.6), it is more difficult to get closed fully before throwing. On fly balls, it is also helpful to catch the ball over your throwing shoulder (figure 5.7). When going back on a fly ball or pop-up, use a "drop step" (figure 5.8). Of course with a backhand (figure 5.9), the body is already closed.

Inside Baseball

Good fielders will get ready for every pitch of the game. Lazy fielders will drift in and out of focus (goon out).

5.5 Before you can throw accurately, you must close off your front side in order to give yourself some direction toward your target.

5.6 When you field a grounder with your hand extended to the forehand side, it takes a real effort to close completely before you throw.

5.7 On fly balls, try to catch the ball over your throwing shoulder.

5.8 When going back on a fly ball or pop-up, use a "drop step"—a step straight back in the anticipated direction of the ball—in order to take a more efficient route to the ball.

5.9 On a backhand play, the body is already closed, and it makes the process much easier.

The throwing motion. Players should be taught to take their heads toward the target (figure 5.10). Most coaches say, "Step toward your target," and although this is good advice, I think it is more effective to think about the head for proper direction.

5.10 Instead of worrying about where you step, just take your head toward the target, and you will step in the direction of your throw.

Paying Attention

The hardest part about all of this is to make sure you prepare on every pitch of the game. It is natural for players to daydream or what I call "goon out" at times during the game and not pay attention. You may be playing right field without having a ball hit to you for six innings, and suddenly there it is, with the game on the line. When you go to a big-league game next time, you will see what I mean. For the most part, every player on the field will be ready on every pitch.

5.11 If you practice, you will be able to transfer the ball in your hand to a cross-seam (or four-seam) grip. Practice getting the grip without looking, and you will eventually be able to do it during games.

Get a Grip

If you are serious about throwing accurately, you should practice gripping the ball across the seams in what is also called a four-seam grip (figure 5.11). Of course this isn't possible on every play, but on most routine plays it is important that you use this grip. As I always tell my students in our school, you have homework: you must watch 30 minutes of television every night for a week. While watching, you simply put on your glove, face it upward, put a ball in it, roll the ball around, and then grab it with the proper grip as fast as you can. You can't look at it as you grip it because you won't be able to look while fielding and throwing a ball during a game. I have seen very young players greatly improve this skill in one week of practicing 30 minutes a night. The next thing you know, you will get a ground ball hit to you, change it in your hand to a four-seam grip, and throw more accurately. This is a good idea if you are an infielder or a catcher, and it is a must if you play the outfield.

> **Tips for Future Pros**
>
> If you get "the thing," whatever you do, keep your sense of humor. If you can laugh at yourself, you can solve any baseball problem.

Hope You Don't Catch "the Thing"

Sometimes, throwing accuracy becomes a mental thing. During the 2000 play-offs, a national television audience watched in horror as Cardinals pitcher Rick Ankiel walked hitters, threw balls to the backstop, and had a total meltdown of his control and/or his emotions. This wasn't a rookie who hadn't had any success but a proven winner, a kid with an unlimited future, a kid who had a very nice delivery. Ankiel was 11–1 for his high school team and struck out 162 hitters in just 74 innings. He signed a contract for $2.5 million with the St. Louis Cardinals. When things unraveled with millions watching, manager Tony LaRussa and pitching coach Dave Duncan were baffled, veteran pitchers shook their heads in disbelief, and baseball fans and purists alike just felt sorry for him. As a former major league pitching coach and a baseball technician since 1972, I tried very hard to spot a flaw in his delivery, and I could not. As the drama unfolded, the scene for me had gone from comical to sad to downright pitiful.

I have seen this scene many times on dimly lit minor league fields during my 35 years in professional baseball. I once saw a pitcher named Wayne White in the Pittsburgh organization who had one of the greatest arms I ever saw just lose control. He would throw a hundred on the side and hit the spots, but he couldn't do the same in a game.

Many baseball fans are familiar with the problems that befell Braves pitcher Mark Wohlers. After posting 97 saves during 1995–1997, he just couldn't find the plate. Noted sports psychologist Jack Llewelyn was called in and gave it his best shot; respected pitching coach Leo Mazzone tried to help; but nobody could find the answer. Wohlers has a great arm, and I'm convinced his problem was not pitching mechanics, for he was even unable to throw to first on bunt plays.

There have been many other instances that affected players but didn't end their careers. One of my favorite pitchers ever was Larry Andersen, who pitched for several major league clubs during the 1980s and 1990s. During the 1990 season I was his pitching coach with the Houston Astros. I admired Larry so much because he had pitched in the minors for 10 years before getting his shot in the big leagues. He then pitched more than 10 seasons in the majors. Larry had developed close to perfect control from the mound as well as one of the best sliders in baseball history. The problem was that Larry couldn't throw to the bases. He hated it when we called for him to throw a pickoff attempt or he had to field a bunt, and so on. He also had a mental block against intentionally walking a hitter. Manager Art Howe and I avoided this situation any way we could. It would have been comical had the game not always been on the line when we had to put a hitter on.

And "the thing" doesn't affect only pitchers. It has happened to major league catchers, even to a couple of second basemen, some of whom were star players at the time. I know of at least three major league catchers who couldn't throw the ball back to the pitcher. Mackey Sasser of the Mets had been a .300 hitter and a competent catcher until 1991 when it hit him. A good friend of mine, Dave Engle, a former Twins catcher, was a converted outfielder, and he caught "the thing" too. He just started lobbing his throws back to the mound until Alfredo Griffin stole a base on one of his soft tosses. He stayed in the majors for nine years and even made the All-Star Team in 1984.

Infielders have caught "the thing" too. Yankees infielder Chuck Knoblauch's problems played out for three seasons and brought him to the brink of retirement at the apex of his career. After being the National League Rookie of the Year in 1982, Dodgers second baseman Steve Sax developed throwing problems during the 1983 season. The fans behind first base only made it worse when they started wearing batting helmets to the game. Sax beat it and returned to become a fine defensive player later in his career.

Everyone who has been in baseball as long as I have, has played and managed in the minor leagues, and has ridden the buses a million miles will know stories like these. How does a player get back on track? The key is getting past the mental blocks that lead to throwing problems.

Get a sports psychologist.   Sports psychologists work. Baseball is a very mental game, and there are many good psychologists working in baseball. One of the best is Fran Pirozzolo, who has worked with the Astros, the Yankees, and many famous golfers and even professional fighters. The key to Pirozzolo's success, I believe, is that he puts a uniform on during practices and becomes one of the players and coaches. He speaks the (baseball) language, and the players like him. Remember, you can't teach someone who doesn't like you.

A success story.   Many pitchers have been wild in the minors and have over-come these kinds of problems with patience, good coaching, and lots of positive reinforcement. When I was with the Astros in 1989, we drafted future All-Star reliever Todd Jones, whom I really believed was one of the wildest college pitchers that I had ever seen.

The day I went to see him in Alabama, he walked or struck out every hitter except the four he hit. The ceiling (up side) was high, but the risk (of Todd being a flop) was considerable. His college coach couldn't even pitch him in games. He would walk hitters, hit hitters, and throw wild pitches in nearly every outing. Scouting director Dan O'Brien let us go out on a limb on the basis of his great arm strength, sharp breaking ball, and good pitcher's body. To add to the pressure, we were able to get Todd as the additional draft pick between the first and second rounds as compensation for the Rangers signing Nolan Ryan. So Todd was known as "the guy that the Astros got for Ryan," and this took its toll in the early years of his career.

Todd was a sensitive kid who got very embarrassed when he got wild. He would feel that he had let the team and the coaches down, and the possibility existed that this could become a real career-threatening problem. We knew that there was risk from the very beginning, and I guess there was a chance that this great talent wouldn't get out of A ball. Pitching coaches Jack Billingham (former Reds Star), Charlie Taylor, and Brent Strom all had a hand in helping Todd overcome his control problems. I think that the thing that turned him around was throwing with his eyes closed on the side with Brent Strom. At Triple-A Tucson, manager Bob Skinner, coach Dave Engle (yes, the same Twins catcher who once had "the thing" himself), and Strom turned Jones's career in the right direction. Had the Astros not traded him to Detroit before his prime, they would have finally had their compensation for the great Nolan Ryan.

Developing Good Defensive Habits

Players have poor defensive habits because they don't practice, they don't have good instruction, or both. Most players talk a good game like, "I love baseball" or "I'm going to make it to the pros," yet they never work at what they say they love. Players can develop quick feet and good hands with hard work. I have seen many players with slow feet, hard hands, and poor arms improve a great deal with the right plan and work ethic. Use of agility drills, plyometrics, jumping rope, and so on will greatly improve your overall quickness and balance. Lots of books are available on these subjects, so get one and start to work.

One of the best drills is one that every player has used at one time or another. To develop good hands and other good habits, throw a tennis ball against the garage, field it properly, change to a four-seam grip, and throw it again (closing off each time). If possible, it is best to paint a target on the garage and try to hit it each time.

> **Inside Baseball**
>
> Get to the ballpark early and watch how many grounders the infielders take before a game. Most big leaguers take 40 to 50 grounders a day and make at least 20 to 25 throws every day in pregame practice.

Make Yourself Work at It

If you are lucky enough to have someone to practice with who is just as dedicated as you are, go to a field and take grounders and fly balls off the bat. Don't let the person hitting to you hit them right at you. Make the fungo hitter move you around from side to side. You are better off working five minutes at game speed and taking a break than you are going half speed for 30 minutes straight. Technique and fundamentals are the only important issues, so pay close attention to opening the glove fully, centering on the ball with your body when possible, closing off, and making accurate throws with the right grip. Take your time and practice sound fundamentals, and you will improve rapidly.

Defense: A Practice Plan for Success for Pros

You can improve at an incredible rate if you do these drills just three times a week for two months.

1. Play catch with a friend for 10 minutes. Take your time and grip the ball correctly across the seams each time you throw. Make sure you keep your eye on the target and never look at the ball while gripping it. Always throw at a target like his glove or his hat, and try to take your

head to the target each time you throw. Play catch at different distances as you get warmed up.

2. Throw each other soft and hard grounders out on the field. Try to get the ball past your buddy. Have fun and put spin on the ball, bet a Coke, and help each other with fundamentals like staying in front of the ball and using the proper positioning. Take 25 apiece and then take a break and do another set.

3. Stand 15 feet apart and throw easy short hops to each other. You can develop good hands with this drill. See how many you can catch without missing.

4. Go to a field and throw pop-ups to each other. Practice using a drop step and going back on balls and setting up properly (see the mechanics section earlier in this chapter).

5. Take sets of 15 grounders off a fungo. Make the fungo hitter force you to work from side to side. Add throwing to the bases if you have the personnel. Take a break after each 15 and talk about your technique and fundamentals.

Playing Good Defense in Games

The most difficult thing about playing good defense during games is learning to stay focused for nine innings. Many times the difference between getting a good jump and a bad jump is just your attention span. It is a tall order to stay ready for 100 to 150 pitches a game. Good players find a way to do this pitch after pitch, inning after inning, and game after game. Part of a scout's job is to watch the jump that players get on the ball. Some players "goon out" as the game proceeds. I have seen outfielders look into the stands or at the ground just before the pitch and get a bad jump because of it.

The game situation will dictate where you position yourself, how aggressively you charge the ball, and your entire approach to the game. Be sure to study the game charts and the game situations later in the book until you are an expert at playing your position.

Game Situations for Defensive Players and Base Coaches

The First Hitter of the Inning

With nobody on and nobody out, the score of the game tells you a lot. The hitter will try to get on base any way possible. He will work the count (see Chapter 3) and try to make the pitcher work and coax a walk out of him. He may still try to bunt for a hit if the infielders play back too far, so just play normal depth at first base and third base. The middle infielders should also just play regular depth. The outfielders should play at normal depth but should be careful not to overcharge singles in front of them. The thought should be to keep the batter-runner (the hitter) at first base. If you are pitching, attack the hitter with strike after strike and get ahead of him.

Things are about the same for the defense when you are behind by more than six runs. Your coach will adjust the positions of the defensive players as the game gets closer. If you are not sure where to play, ask the coach.

If the score is tied or at least very close, your coach may want the corner infielders to guard the line (a step and a dive off the line) to prevent doubles. If you are the third baseman and the hitter at the plate can run, you will want to play even with the bag to prevent a bunt for a base hit. If you are playing the outfield, you should also play three or four steps deeper to prevent the ball from going over your head for extra bases.

> **Tips for Future Pros**
>
> Good players learn to "rehearse" each play before it happens (while in the "thinking position," as in figure 5.1). Each player should ask himself, "What will I do if the ball is hit to me right now?" This applies to *every* pitch of every game you play.

Situation A: Nobody on base, no outs

Catcher: Is everyone on the defense playing this hitter correctly? Start with a fastball away, get strike one, and work from there. If there is a ground ball hit to the right side, get over and back up the throw at first base.

Pitcher: Get ahead in the count, and keep the ball down. With any ball hit to the first-base side, get over and cover first base.

Third baseman: Can this hitter run? If so, play in for a possible bunt.

Shortstop: Are all of the defensive players playing this hitter correctly? Watch for the signs, and if an off-speed pitch is called, expect the ball to be hit toward the third-base hole.

Second baseman: Same as the shortstop, plus play in a step or two if the hitter is an above-average runner.

First baseman: Play deep in order to get all the range that you can. Remind the pitcher to cover first base if a ball is hit to the first-base side of the field.

Leftfielder: Make sure that you are playing this hitter correctly. If the centerfielder moves left or right, move the same number of steps.

Centerfielder: You are the key to the outfield defense. Know how to play each hitter and also make sure that the left- and rightfielders move with you. If the pitcher gets behind in the count, back up two steps. Move in if he gets ahead in the count.

Rightfielder: Back up all throws to first base made by the pitcher, catcher, shortstop, and third baseman.

Third-base coach: Is the third baseman playing back too far? If he is, consider asking the hitter to bunt. Can you see the pitcher tipping his pitches? Is the catcher covering up his signs?

First-base coach: Can you see the signs from the catcher? Is the pitcher tipping his pitches?

Two Outs and Nobody on Base

About the same as the above except the first and third baseman can play deeper and let them have the bunt single.

A Stealing Situation

If you are playing first base, hold the runner on, and if he breaks you must let the catcher and everyone else know by yelling "Runner!" or "There he goes!" or whatever your club uses. When a steal is in order, one of the middle infielders must decide who is going to cover on the steal before the pitch is made. If you are the most experienced player of the two, you will most likely call the coverage. If you are calling the play, you simply look at the hitter at the plate and decide where to play the hitter.

After you arrive in position, you will hold your glove up to your mouth and show your middle infield partner the coverage. If you show him a closed mouth it means that you will cover, and if you show him an open mouth, it means that he should cover. You make the decision based mostly on the hitter being left-handed or right-handed. For a left-handed hitter, the second baseman will probably play toward first base a few steps so the shortstop will cover second. If there is a right-handed hitter, it will be just the opposite and the second baseman will cover. In higher baseball the coverage may change based on the pitch, but this is simply not necessary at the lower levels.

> **Tips for Future Pros**
>
> On tag plays (steals and others), infielders must block the ball in the dirt and prevent it from going into the outfield. There is no excuse for letting through a ball that is thrown low.

If the runner goes and you are covering, don't just sprint straight to the bag, for you will vacate your position too soon. Try charging two steps toward the hitter and then turn to cover the bag. You will still be at the bag in plenty of time.

When you approach the bag to cover, place your left foot in the rear of the bag and straddle it. Some baseball people will say that the infielder should place his foot in front of the bag, but I disagree. I think that most infielders will reach in front for the throw instead of waiting for the ball. It is a proven fact that this method is slower when you reach out, receive the ball, and return to the bag to make the tag.

When the runner slides in, you simply place your glove in front of the bag and the runner will slide into your glove. Keep the back of your glove toward the runner so that he can't kick the ball loose and you won't get hurt.

Situation B: Runner on first, fewer than two outs

Catcher: Is this a situation in which they might start the runner? What can you call to get the hitter to hit a grounder?

Pitcher: You need a grounder now. A good fastball down in the zone would be perfect. Who is covering second base if a ball is hit back to you? Is this a fast runner on first who is apt to steal?

Third baseman: If a grounder is hit to you, throw to second base for a force.

Shortstop: Take two steps toward second base (cheat) for the double play. If there is a left-handed hitter up, cover on the steal or hit-and-run. Also cover second base if a ball is hit back to the pitcher. Remind the pitcher before the play that you will cover second base. If a grounder is hit to you, throw to second base for the double-play attempt (a good, firm chest-high throw).

Second baseman: Cheat over toward the bag two steps for the double play. If the ball is hit directly at you or to your right, throw to second base for the double play. If the ball is hit to your left and you have to extend for it, throw to first base and just get the batter out.

First baseman: Hold the runner on first. As the pitcher delivers to the plate, get off the line two steps in order to cover your position. If the runner is the tying or winning run late in the game, and because the runner can score from second base down the line, stay put in order to protect against a double down the right-field line.

Leftfielder: If there is a base hit to you, throw to third base. If the ball is hit to you in the air, throw to second base. If the ball goes over your head or in the gap, come up and hit the cutoff man (the shortstop).

Centerfielder: On a base hit to you, throw the ball to third base. If the ball is over your head or in the gap, retrieve the ball and throw it to the cutoff man.

Rightfielder: If there is a base hit to you, throw toward third base to the shortstop, who will be the cutoff man in line with third base. If the ball is hit down the line, in the right-center-field gap, or over your head, retrieve the ball and hit the cutoff man.

Third-base coach: Are both the hitter and the baserunner at first base watching the signs? Is the pitcher slow to the plate from the stretch? Is this a good time for a steal? How about a hit-and-run?

First-base coach: Does this pitcher have a good move? If he does, remind the runner. Also remind the runner on first of the outs and the game situation at least twice if he is a smart baserunner and after every pitch if he is not.

Situation C: Runner on first with two outs

Catcher: Is this a situation in which they might start the runner? What can you call to get the hitter to hit a grounder?

Pitcher: Keep the ball down. It is important to get ahead in the count. A good fastball down in the zone would be perfect right now. Is there a fast runner on first likely to steal second base?

Third baseman: If a grounder is hit to you, throw to second base for a force.

Shortstop: If there is a left-handed hitter up, cover on the steal or hit-and-run. If a grounder is hit to you, throw to second base for the third out. Remember that if the runner is running on the pitch or if it is a slow-hit ball, go to first base for the out.

Second baseman: If the ball is hit at you or to your right, throw to second base for the force. If the ball is hit to your left and you have to extend for it, throw to first base and just get the out. If there is a right-handed hitter up, you have the coverage on the steal.

First baseman: Hold the runner on first. As the pitcher delivers to the plate, get off the line two steps in order to cover your position. If the runner is the tying or winning run late in the game, and because the runner can score from second base down the line, stay put in order to protect against the double down the right-field line.

Leftfielder: If there is a base hit to you, throw to third base. If the ball is hit to you in the air, throw to second base. If the ball goes over your head or in the gap, come up and hit the cutoff man (the shortstop).

Centerfielder: On a base hit to you, throw the ball to third base. If the ball is over your head or in the gap, retrieve the ball and throw to the cutoff man.

Rightfielder: If there is a base hit to you, throw toward third base to the shortstop, who will be the cutoff man in line with third base. If the ball is hit down the line, in the right-center-field gap, or over your head, retrieve the ball and hit the cutoff man.

Third-base coach: Are both the hitter and the baserunner at first base watching the signs? Is the pitcher slow to the plate from the stretch? Is this a good time for a steal?

First-base coach: Does this pitcher have a good move? If he does, remind the runner. Also remind the runner on first of the outs and the game situation at least twice if he is a smart baserunner and after every pitch if he is not.

Man on Second, No Outs

The hitter is going to (or should try to) hit the ball on the ground to the right side. He will probably wait for a pitch (usually a fastball) on that side of the plate. If you are playing first base, you should play a couple of steps off the line with a left-handed hitter and straight up with a right-handed hitter. If you are playing second base and there is a right-handed hitter up, you will have to keep an eye on the runner on second so you will play a couple of steps toward the bag. If a left-handed hitter is up, you will protect the hole toward first base. If you're the shortstop and a left-handed hitter is up, you will watch the runner on second and position yourself a couple of steps toward the bag. With a right-handed hitter up, you will play straight up. The third baseman will play straight up and be alive for a play at third should the ball be hit to short or back to the pitcher. The out-fielders play a couple of steps toward right field until there are two strikes on the hitter. After two strikes, the hitter will just try to put the ball in play anywhere so the outfielders will return to straight up.

Situation D: Runner on second

Catcher: Go out and remind the pitcher to keep the ball down. Block everything in the dirt.

Pitcher: Pitch out of the stretch and keep the runner close at second base. If you do a good job keeping him close, your teammates might have a chance to throw him out at home.

Third baseman: Play as deep as you can and still get to third base in case of a steal.

Shortstop: If a right-handed hitter bats, play very deep. With a left-handed hitter up, you have some responsibility to hold the runner or at least keep him close.

Second baseman: Play very deep if there is a left-handed hitter at the plate. With a right-handed hitter up, you have some responsibility to hold the runner or at least keep him close.

First baseman: Play very deep and knock the ball down to make sure of an out.

Leftfielder: If there is a base hit to you, throw to home. If the ball is hit to you in the air, throw to third base. If the ball goes over your head or in the gap, come up and hit the cutoff man (the shortstop).

Centerfielder: On a base hit to you, throw the ball to home. If a fly ball is hit to you, throw to third. If the ball is over your head or in the gap, retrieve the ball and throw to the cutoff man.

Rightfielder: If there is a base hit to you, throw the ball to home. If a fly ball is hit to you, throw to third. If the ball is down the line, in the right-center-field gap, or over your head, retrieve the ball and hit the cutoff man.

Third-base coach: Are the hitter and the baserunner at second base watching the signs? Watch the shortstop and the second baseman for a possible pickoff attempt. Know the arm strength of the outfielders. What does the potential run on base represent?

First-base coach: You have no real responsibilities.

Man on Third, Infield Plays In

The infielders will all play on the cut of the grass to cut off the run at the plate. Because the game will be close in this situation, it is important that all infielders take their time and make good throws. If the ball is hit medium to sharply, the runner will most likely freeze and return to third. After fielding the ball, you should look the runner back to third and throw to first for the out.

Situation E: Runner on third or runners on first and third, fewer than two outs, infield in

Catcher: Go out and remind the pitcher to keep the ball down. Block everything in the dirt.

Pitcher: Pitch out of the stretch and make sure you come to a complete stop at the belt. Keep the ball down because a deep fly ball can score a run.

Third baseman: Play two steps behind the baseline, charge everything on the ground, and throw to home.

Shortstop: Play two steps behind the baseline, charge everything on the ground, and throw to home (with a good, firm, chest-high throw).

Second baseman: Play two steps behind the baseline, charge everything on the ground, and throw to home.

First baseman: Hold the runner on first. As the pitcher delivers to the plate, get off the line two steps in order to cover your position. If the runner is the tying or winning run late in the game, and because the runner can score from second base down the line, stay put in order to protect against the double down the right-field line.

Leftfielder: If there is a base hit to you, throw to second base. If the ball is hit to you in the air, throw to home. If the ball goes over your head or in the gap, come up and hit the cutoff man (the shortstop).

Centerfielder: On a base hit to you, throw the ball to second base. If the fly ball is hit to you, throw to home. Be careful to hit the cutoff man (the first baseman). If the ball is over your head or in the gap, retrieve the ball and throw to the cutoff man.

Rightfielder: If there is a base hit to you, throw the ball to second base. If a fly ball is hit to you, throw to home. Be careful to hit the cutoff man (the first baseman). If the ball is down the line, in the right-center-field gap, or over your head, retrieve the ball and hit the cutoff man.

Third-base coach: Is this the time for a squeeze play? Where are the infielders playing? If they are in, tell the runner on third base to make the ball be through. Remind him to freeze on a line drive.

First-base coach: You have no real responsibilities.

Situation F: Runner on third or runners on first and third, fewer than two outs, big lead, infield back

Catcher: Go out and remind the pitcher to keep the ball down. Block everything in the dirt.

Pitcher: Pitch out of the stretch and make sure you come to a complete stop at the belt. Keep the ball down and throw strikes. The other club will have to hit their way on base. Your most important job is to get strike one and stay ahead in the count. If the ball is hit back to you, don't panic, but get an out somewhere.

Third baseman: Play two steps behind the baseline, and throw either to second for the force or to first, but you must get an out on this play.

Shortstop: Play as deep as you can, depending on the speed of the runner at the plate. Get an out somewhere to help prevent a big inning.

Second baseman: Play deep, and get an out somewhere.

First baseman: Find out if the manager wants you to hold the runner on first. If you play behind him, throw to second only if you have a clear shot and the runner is an easy out. If not, take the easy out at first or throw to the pitcher covering.

Leftfielder: If there is a base hit to you, throw to second base. If the ball is hit to you in the air, throw to second unless you have the runner dead at home. If the ball goes over your head or in the gap, come up and hit the cutoff man (the shortstop).

Centerfielder: On a base hit to you, throw the ball to second base. If a fly ball is hit to you, throw to home only if the runner is an easy out. Be careful to hit the cutoff man (the first baseman). If the ball is over your head or in the gap, retrieve the ball and throw to the cutoff man.

Rightfielder: If there is a base hit to you, throw the ball to second base. Throw home on a fly ball to you only if the runner is an easy out. Be careful to hit the cutoff man (the first baseman). If the ball is down the line, in the right-center-field gap, or over your head, retrieve the ball and hit the cutoff man.

Third-base coach: Don't let any runners run into easy outs. Where are the infielders playing? If they are in, tell the runner on third base to make the ball be through. Remind him to freeze on a line drive.

First-base coach: Because the first baseman may play behind the runner, watch him closely. The last thing you need is to have a runner picked off when your club is down so many runs.

Situation G: Runners on first and third, fewer than two outs, close game, corner infielders back, and middle infielders playing for double play

Catcher: Go out and remind the pitcher to keep the ball down. Block everything in the dirt.

Pitcher: Know who is covering second base on a ball hit back to you. If the ball is hit back to you, throw to second base and turn a double play after checking the runner at third base. Pitch out of the stretch and make sure you come to a complete stop at the belt. Keep the ball down and throw strikes, for a ground ball (a double play) will get you out of trouble.

Third baseman: Play one step behind the baseline. On a ball hit to your left, throw to second for the double play; on a ball hit near the bag, tag the bag and throw to first; on a slow-hit ball, throw to home or first.

Shortstop: Play at double-play depth and try and turn this double play. If the ball is hit very slowly, go to first and get an out. Cover on the steal with a runner on first and a left-handed hitter up.

Second baseman: Play at double-play depth and turn a double play. Cover second with a runner on first with a steal and a right-handed hitter up.

First baseman: Hold the runner on first. If the ball is hit to you, throw to the shortstop for the double play.

Leftfielder: If there is a base hit to you, throw to the shortstop, who is the cutoff man to third. If the ball is hit to you in the air, throw to home making sure to hit the cutoff man (the third baseman). If the ball goes over your head or in the gap, come up and hit the cutoff man (the shortstop).

Centerfielder: If there is a base hit to you, throw to the shortstop, who is the cutoff man to third. If the ball is hit to you in the air, throw to home making sure to hit the cutoff man (the first baseman). If the ball goes over your head or in the gap, come up and hit the cutoff man (the shortstop).

Rightfielder: If there is a base hit to you, throw to the shortstop, who is the cutoff man to third. If the ball is hit to you in the air, throw to home making sure to hit the cutoff man (the first baseman). If the ball goes over your head or in the gap, come up and hit the cutoff man (the shortstop).

Third-base coach: Where are the infielders playing? If they are in, tell the runner on third base to make the ball be through. Remind him to freeze on a line drive. If there is no out, tell the runner to wait until the third baseman throws to second base for the double play before he goes.

First-base coach: Because the first baseman may play behind the runner, watch him closely. The last thing you need is to have a runner picked off when your club is down so many runs.

Man on Third, Infield Plays Back

We probably have a big lead with this alignment, so unless the ball is hit to third or very hard to first base on the ground, we will give up a run for an out on defense. Everyone will play normal depth and straight up and just get the out at first. The exception is when the ball is hit back to the pitcher. The third baseman must be alert in case the runner makes a mistake and gets hung up in a rundown.

> **Inside Baseball**
> If there is a tag play at the plate, notice where the catcher places his left foot in preparation to block the runner off the plate as he receives the ball.

Double Play Situation

The pitcher should look back at the middle infielders and find out who is covering second on the ball hit back to him. The first baseman should make sure of one out by making a good throw over the bag to the shortstop. When the return throw is made, he should receive the throw if possible, but the pitcher may run him off and cover if the ground ball takes the first baseman too far from the bag. The middle infielders must "cheat" over into double-play depth by taking two steps toward the bag and two steps in. If the ball is slowly hit, they must charge hard, forget the double play, and just get the out at first. If the runners are on first and second, the third baseman has the option of tagging third and throwing to first if the ball is hit near the bag or going to the second baseman covering second for the force out.

Situation H: Runners on first and second, no outs, game not close, no bunt in order

Catcher: Is this a situation in which they might start the runner? What can you call to get the hitter to hit a grounder?

Pitcher: You need a grounder now. A good fastball down in the zone would be perfect. Who is covering second base if a ball is hit back to you? Is this a fast runner on first who is apt to steal?

Third baseman: If a grounder is hit to you, throw to second base for a force. Or, on a ball hit near the bag, you may elect to tag third base and throw to first base.

Shortstop: Take two steps toward second base (cheat) for the double play. If there is a left-handed hitter up, cover on the steal or hit-and-run. Also cover second base if a ball is hit back to the pitcher. Remind the pitcher before the play that you will cover second base. If a grounder is hit to you, throw to second base for the double play.

Second baseman: Cheat over toward the bag two steps for the double play. If the ball is hit at you or to your right, throw to second base for the double play. If the ball is hit to your left and you have to extend for it, throw to first base and just get the out.

First baseman: Play behind the runner, and be alert for any pickoff plays that your team might have. If the ball is hit at you on the ground or to your right, throw the ball to the shortstop covering second base for the potential double play. Try to get to first base for the return throw, but if you can't get there, the pitcher will cover.

Leftfielder: If there is a base hit to you, throw to home. If the ball is hit to you in the air, throw to third base. If the ball goes over your head or in the gap, come up and hit the cutoff man (the shortstop).

Centerfielder: On a base hit to you, throw the ball to home and hit the cutoff man (the first baseman). If the ball is over your head or in the gap, retrieve the ball and throw to the cutoff man.

Rightfielder: If there is a base hit to you, throw to home to the cutoff man (first baseman). If the ball is down the line, in the right-center-field gap, or over your head, retrieve the ball and hit the cutoff man.

Third-base coach: Are the hitter and the baserunners at first base and second base watching the signs? Watch the shortstop and second baseman for a possible pickoff attempt. Know the arm strength of the outfielders. What do the potential runs on base represent?

First-base coach: Watch the first baseman closely and make sure he doesn't come in behind the runner for a pickoff attempt.

Man on First, Sacrifice Bunt in Order (See Situation B)

If you're an infielder, you should run over in your head whatever bunt plays that your team has prior to the play. If you are unsure of the plays, ask somebody;

don't try to fake it. Remember that the hitter's job is to bunt the ball to the first-base side because the third baseman will be charging early. If you are playing first base, you should hold the runner on, then charge the plate when the pitcher delivers to home. If you're playing second, you will cheat a few steps toward first and cover first if the ball is bunted. The shortstop covers second. If you're playing third base, you will position yourself a couple of steps in front of the baseline, then charge hard when the hitter shows bunt. The catcher must come out quickly, for he may have to field the bunt. If you're the catcher, you must call the play for all of the infielders (tell them whether to throw to first or second) and then cover third base if the third baseman doesn't get back to cover. The outfielders should back up second and first, depending on the angle (the throwing lane) that is established by the throw.

> **Inside Baseball**
> Watch the second baseman and shortstop reposition themselves closer to the bag and farther in at "double-play depth." This makes it easier for them to arrive at the bag in time to turn a double play. They will also make eye contact with the pitcher to let him know who is covering if a ball is hit back to him.

If you are the pitcher, you come set, check the runner, and deliver a strike to the plate. Your coverage is straight ahead, and you should listen for the catcher to call the play.

Man on First and Second, Sacrifice Bunt in Order

Major league teams have three different bunt defenses for this situation. Normally this is a close game and the defense will make or break the game depending on what happens on this play. The manager or coach will give the sign for the play to the third baseman, and he will give the sign to the rest of the infield. Most of the time, the sign will be the last thing he touches with his right hand or the first touch after he touches his hat. These are universal, and most clubs keep the same signs all season long.

The hitter will try to bunt the ball to third base and make the third baseman field the ball. The job of the defense is simple: you must get an out. If you can get the guy at third, great, but if you can't, you must get an out at first. If you fail at this task, your club will be facing a bases-loaded and no-out situation.

Regular coverage: play 1.   The pitcher delivers the ball and covers the third-base line. If you are playing first base, you will position yourself in the baseline then charge hard when the hitter shows bunt. If you field the ball quickly and have your feet underneath you (you just can't throw the ball away), then take a shot at third to force the runner (you will be listening to the catcher, who is calling the play for everyone). If there is any doubt in your mind about getting the runner at third, stop, set yourself, and throw it to the second baseman covering first.

The second baseman will cover first. If you're the shortstop, you are the key to the play. You will come in right behind the runner and hold him close with a fake or two, then cover second if the bunt is made. Remember that the hitter may fake a bunt and hit (slash) with a half swing, so hold your ground and don't break toward second until you see the bunt made. If the hitter makes a really bad bunt, your team may turn a double play. Also be heads up in case the hitter bunts through (misses) the pitch, for the runner might take a couple steps toward third and the catcher can pick him off with you covering second.

If you are playing third, you will hold your ground in the baseline and make a decision whether the pitcher can field the ball or not. If he can't get it (he won't get it unless they make a poor bunt), then you must charge hard, field the ball, and get an out at first. Remember that if you run the pitcher off and get the out at first, your club is still OK. The catcher calls the play, and the outfielders back up first, second, and third.

If you are the pitcher, you come set, look at the shortstop, who is behind the runner, and deliver a strike to the plate. Your coverage is straight to the third-base line (listen for the catcher). Remember that you must get an out on this play. The runner may be getting a big lead off second, and if he does, just step off. I always say, "Don't run a bad play." If you don't like what you see behind you (at second base), just step off and kill the play.

Situation I: Runners on first and second, no outs, game close, bunt in order, regular coverage—play 1

Catcher: Get the sign from the third baseman. Watch the pitcher fielding the ball, and make the call for the play to go to first base or third base. Be sure to call third base, for getting an out at first base is not that bad in this situation. If the hitter bunts through the ball, the runner on second base may be hung out to dry, and he can be picked off after the pitch.

Pitcher: Get the sign from the third baseman. Come set, look at the shortstop, and let him make a two-step break toward third. Deliver a strike, and field the third-base line when the hitter bunts. Listen for the catcher to let you know if the ball should go to third base or first base. While going for the ball, if you hear the third baseman call it, let him make the play to first base.

Third baseman: Get the sign from the manager, and give it to the rest of the players. Play in the baseline a couple of steps from third. When the pitcher comes set and the hitter shows bunt, watch the pitcher cover the line. If he can't get the ball, come hard, field it, and throw to first base for the out. If you are sure the pitcher can get it quickly, cover third base as he throws it to third base to force the lead runner.

Shortstop: Get the sign from the third baseman. Set up directly behind the runner on second base and wait until the pitcher comes set. Fake a couple of steps toward third, and hold your position. When the ball is bunted, cover second base. If the hitter bunts through the ball, the catcher may be able to pick him off after the pitch.

Second baseman: Get the sign from the third baseman. Cheat over toward the bag two steps for the double play. Make a bluff toward second to freeze the runner, and then break toward first base and cover first.

First baseman: Play in the baseline or a couple of steps in front. When the pitcher delivers the ball, charge very hard and cover the first-base line and the middle.

Leftfielder: Back up the possible throw to third once the ball is bunted.

Centerfielder: Back up the possible throw to second base on either a bunt or a possible pickoff from the catcher.

Rightfielder: Back up the possible play at first base.

Third-base coach: Watch the runner on second, and protect him from the pickoff attempt.

First-base coach: Watch the first baseman closely, and make sure he doesn't come in behind the runner for a pickoff attempt.

The wheel play.   The object of this play is to get the out at third. Your team is gambling first that the hitter is bunting for sure, and second that they will in fact get the lead runner at third. If you are playing short, you are again the key to the play. You initially come in behind the runner as you did in the regular coverage, but when the pitcher comes set, you break hard to third and cover the base.

If you're playing third, you start the play even with the baseline and charge hard when the shortstop has a couple of steps' lead on the runner. If you field the ball quickly, you will probably be able to get the runner at third; if not, just get the out at first. The pitcher comes set, watches the shortstop, and delivers a strike when he has a couple of steps' lead on the runner going to third. The pitcher has the coverage straight ahead.

Situation J: Runners on first and second, no outs, game close, bunt in order—the wheel play

Catcher: Get the sign from the third baseman. Watch the pitcher fielding the ball, and make the call for the play to go to first base or third base. Be sure to call third base, for getting an out at first base is not that bad in this situation. If the hitter bunts through the ball, you have no play at second base because there is nobody covering.

Pitcher: Get the sign from the third baseman. Come set, look at the shortstop, and watch him break toward third base. When he has a two-step lead on the runner, deliver a strike and field straight ahead when the hitter bunts. This play is set up to get the force at third base.

> **Inside Baseball**
>
> The third baseman will give the sign for the coverage. Watch the shortstop, for his movements will let you know which play the defense is using.

Third baseman: Get the sign from the manager, and give it to the rest of the players. Play in the baseline a couple of steps from third. When the pitcher comes set and the hitter shows bunt, charge the ball hard, field it, and throw to the shortstop covering third base.

Shortstop: Get the sign from the third baseman. Set up directly behind the runner on second base, and wait until the pitcher comes set. Break for third base and cover third base for the force. If the runner breaks with you initially, call for the pitcher to step off and kill the play.

Second baseman: Get the sign from the third baseman. Cheat over toward the bag two steps for the double play. Make a bluff toward second to freeze the runner, then break toward first base to cover first.

First baseman: Play in the baseline or a couple of steps in front. When the pitcher delivers the ball, charge very hard, cover the first-base line, and make the throw to third base for the force of the lead runner.

Leftfielder: Back up the possible throw to third once the ball is bunted.

Centerfielder: Charge hard for the possibility that the runner on second might get hung up between second base and third base.

Rightfielder: Back up the possible play at first base.

Third-base coach: Watch the runner on second, and protect him from the pickoff attempt. Watch the third baseman to see if you can catch the signs. It is usually the last touch or the touch after the hat that indicates the bunt play is on.

First-base coach: Watch the third baseman to see if you can catch the signs. It is usually the last touch or the touch after the hat that indicates the bunt play is on. Watch for the ball to be popped up.

The pickoff play. Everything is the same as the wheel play. If you are the short-stop, you make the same move toward third. If you are the second baseman, you take one step toward first and then break back to second for the pickoff. If you are the pitcher, you wait for the shortstop to break for third and then turn and throw to the second baseman covering second. If you don't have a play, don't throw. One of the keys is that the entire defense does a good job of acting and makes this play look like the wheel play.

Keep in mind that the "daylight play" is always on. If the infielder can sneak in behind a runner and get daylight between himself and the runner, he will flash the open glove as a signal for the pitcher to pivot and throw. Some clubs also use a sign to put on a timed pickoff play. The pitcher or infielder will pick at his uniform or rub a body part to put on the play, and his partner will answer with a pick or a rub to confirm the sign. This play is a timed play that is normally a one-second count after the pitcher turns his head toward home. Either player can put on the play.

Situation K: Runners on first and second, no outs, game close, bunt in order—the pickoff play

Catcher: The third baseman gives the sign for the play. Give a sign, a good target, and everything to make the offense think the wheel play is on.

Pitcher: The third baseman gives the sign for the play. Come set, look at the shortstop, and watch him break toward third base. When the runner takes the fake, turn and throw to the second baseman for the pickoff. If you don't have a play, don't throw. If the play doesn't develop properly, step off and kill the play.

Third baseman: Get the sign from the manager, and give it to the rest of the players. Play in the baseline a couple of steps from third. When the pitcher comes set and the hitter shows bunt, charge a couple of steps to make this play look like the wheel play.

Shortstop: The third baseman gives the sign for the play. Do everything to make this look like the wheel play. Set up directly behind the runner on second base, and wait until the pitcher comes set. Break for third base just as you would on the wheel play.

Second baseman: The third baseman gives the sign for the play. Cheat over toward the bag two steps for the double play. Fake toward first base and then break to second base for the pickoff.

First baseman: Play in the baseline or a couple of steps in front. When the pitcher delivers the ball, charge very hard, cover the first-base line, and make the throw to third base for the force of the lead runner.

Leftfielder: Back up the possible throw to third once the ball is bunted.

Centerfielder: Charge hard for the possibility that the runner on second might get hung up between second base and third base.

Rightfielder: Back up the possible play at first base.

Third-base coach: Watch the runner on second and protect him from the pickoff attempt. Watch the third baseman to see if you can catch the signs. It is usually the last touch or the touch after the hat that indicates the bunt play is on.

First-base coach: Watch the third baseman to see if you can catch the signs. It is usually the last touch or the touch after the hat that indicates the bunt play is on. Watch for the ball to be popped up.

Runners on First and Third—Double Steal

Some managers will try to steal a run in this situation. They will have the runner break for second and stop halfway when the defense throws the ball to second. The runner on third breaks for the plate, and the defense can't get the ball back to home soon enough. This is really a Little League play, and in higher ball it should never work, but it does.

There are lots of trick plays that the defense can use. Some defensive clubs will fake a throw to second to try and trap the runner off third, while others throw the ball back to the pitcher to accomplish the same thing.

The best defense is to have the catcher come up, make a quick look to third, and throw to second. One middle infielder stays on the base for the tag, and the other comes up in front to cut off the ball and relay it to the plate if the runner on third breaks. I think that when there is a slow runner on third, you should always throw to second.

Other Defensive Plays

Pop-Ups Between the Infield and the Outfield

The infielder should go hard after the ball and keep going until he hears the outfielder call him off. The outfielder should be very aggressive and vocal to both catch the ball and protect both players from collisions. Players of all ages can be injured severely in collisions. A shortstop from the Pirates' organization died in Salem, Virginia, from a collision with the leftfielder on such a pop-up.

Potential Squeeze

The situation for a potential squeeze should be obvious. There will be a runner on third or runners on first and third with one out. Nobody does it with no outs and certainly not with two outs. The game must be close, and the hitter at the plate is usually not a great hitter. Some managers use the "safety" squeeze, which requires the runner on third to see the ball on the ground and then break for home (see Chapter 6). With the "suicide" squeeze, the runner breaks when the pitcher commits to the plate.

If you are the pitcher, you must go from a stretch (even if there is just a runner on third). The runner will go when your arm starts forward or your front foot hits, so check him early and then don't worry about it. Your first job is always to get the hitter out. If you are the third baseman, you will keep an eye on the runner at third. Because most clubs will actually tell the runner on third (with a word sign) that the squeeze is on, you should go right next to the bag and listen. Some other coaches will use a touch like grabbing the elbow of the runner when the play is on. If the runner breaks early, you must yell "Runner" or "There he goes" or whatever is prearranged with your club. If the pitcher hears it in time, he throws whatever pitch is called away from the hitter. If you are the catcher and the runner breaks early, simply jump out into the other batter's box (away), receive the ball, and tag the runner out. If the runner leaves that early, he will usually have to stop, and a rundown will develop. If you are playing left field, you will back up third. Everyone else plays regular defense.

> **Tips for Future Pros**
>
> Practice your fielding mechanics until you no longer have to think about the movements. Throw or hit grounders and fly balls with a friend, or throw the ball against a wall if you have to. Big-league infielders typically practiced throwing a ball against a wall for hours when they were kids. Most players take between 50 and 100 grounders a day during the season.

Profiles of Great Defensive Players

Born to Play Short (Alan Trammell)

Alan Trammell was a terrific athlete. He was a superb basketball player in high school and a natural as a defensive player. His hands even looked good at Kearny High School in San Diego on a very bad field where I first scouted him. His coach, the late Jack Taylor, was a friend of mine and told me to come see this great kid he had playing shortstop. I learned a big lesson as a scout in 1976 when I didn't have the guts to take him earlier in the draft. Dick Wienck of the Detroit Tigers took him in the second round, which was way before anybody else would have (he also signed Mark McGwire). I guess he saw a potential great hitter as well as a great fielder in this very skinny kid with long hair and a very competitive attitude. Everyone saw the great hands, but a hitter who would drive in more than 1,000 runs? No, I didn't think so. Six All-Star teams, four Gold Gloves, and 20 years in the majors later, Dick was right and everyone else who scouted San Diego in those years just missed, including me. I did salvage the year by drafting Dave Smith (216 saves, lifetime) in the eighth round out of San Diego State. I have learned a lot about scouting from Dick, Dave Garcia, Jack Bloomfield, Harry Minor, Gary Sutherland, Jerry Gardner, and other great scouts.

He Can Play Anywhere (Ivan "Pudge" Rodriguez)

Pudge could have been a shortstop, a centerfielder, or anything else that he wanted to be. He is one of those players who come along only once in a while. His defensive skills are right up there with Johnny Bench's, but I think his quickness goes beyond Bench and anyone else that I have ever seen. Remember that we said that defensive players field with their feet? Well, Pudge is a perfect example. Sure, genetics are on his side, but he works very hard on his legs and feet. During the winter, he has a four-month program with a track coach. This program includes running sprints, running around cones, leaping over boxes for agility, and jumping—lots and lots of jumping. Catching takes its toll on a body, and this guy catches more games than anyone else. I believe he might be in better shape legwise than anyone in baseball.

Advance scouts just tell their clubs to forget the running game when playing against him. He makes the runners stay close so that his team can turn more double plays. His opponents can't score on some doubles from first and can't score from second or go from first to third on singles.

His defensive contributions don't stop there. He calls a great game for his pitcher and his team. He understands game situations as well as anyone and knows the weaknesses and tendencies of his opponents. Rodriguez blocks pitches in the dirt and is without peer as far as fielding bunts.

One criticism I would make is that in recent years he has not been as involved with his pitchers as he should be, and his game calling has slipped. The only other real hole in his game is the fact that he doesn't block the plate on tag plays very well.

The Perfect Gold Glover (Steve Finley)

No other defensive player has better balance and body control than Steve Finley has. He has no peer in baseball going back on balls. Nobody charges grounders or has better accuracy than "Fins." There are better arms (Andruw Jones) than his, but accuracy and smart play are his trademarks. Why? He works at it. I have watched him and Luis Gonzalez practice great plays, while other outfielders like Griffey and Bonds just show up and play.

If you watch him during batting practice or during spring training, you'll see that he is constantly working on the skills necessary to be a great defensive player. You would think that after several Gold Gloves he would relax and let his skills take care of everything. It is just the opposite. He is working harder every year, for he wants to play into his forties. For a baseball purist like me, the angles or routes that he takes to the ball are incredible. It is not just luck when he turns away from the ball, runs to a spot, and the ball seems to arrive the same time as he does. The sad thing about all of this is that he has always been a Gold Glove player, but until he began hitting home runs, nobody noticed.

Hit Me Another Bucket (Kenny Rogers)

Talk about hard work. This is what Kenny Rogers and his Gold Glove is all about. During spring training of 1998 when I was his pitching coach, I hit him thousands of balls. He would seek me out at the end of the day and ask me to hit balls back at him as hard as I could, bucket after bucket, until near dark. I would smoke balls back at him from home plate. When one would get by him, he would get mad at himself and want more and more. I am six foot two and weigh 230 pounds and can hit a fungo very hard, but he would tell me, "Come on, you can hit harder than that." I was always concerned that I would kill our ace pitcher.

Along with great defensive skills, he has a great pickoff move (which is a result of more hard work) and a great feel for the game. No other pitcher that I was around had a better understanding of game situations.

Running and Thinking

The Mechanics

Most baseball players run very badly in a mechanical sense. Some swing their arms across their bodies instead of pumping them correctly at their sides, causing them to lose an inch or two of distance on every stride. Most don't have the forward body lean to run to first as fast as they could, and few work on the proper weight training that could potentially increase their speed. Professional baseball is full of guys who need help with their running mechanics, and this goes largely unnoticed by most organizations.

In 1983, as the director of player development of the San Diego Padres, I brought a track coach to spring training. Even though he taught the fastest runners how to steal bases more effectively and taught everyone to run faster and more efficiently, I was told by "old-school" general manager Jack McKeon that there was no money to pay a running coach. Not much has changed in the past 20 years. Running coaches are few and far between in pro baseball, and the mechanics are still poor. If you are serious about being the best baseball player that you can be, buy a book on running mechanics and apply the programs. It will help you defensively and offensively.

Developing as a Baserunner

Former major league manager Bill Virdon once told me, "Running the bases is the thing that all fans use to judge the effort that a player is giving." When you think about it, you realize that it is very true. Every person in the ballpark, regardless of his or her knowledge of the game, appreciates a player who runs hard or dives into a base in an effort to beat the play. Conversely, fans, media, other players, coaches, and so on notice when a player loafs to first. In Bill's era, everyone ran the ball out or the other players got all over him. It was the accepted way to play baseball from high school to the majors. That is no longer true. I watch more than two hundred big-league games a year. It has gotten to the point where only one or two teams will collectively run the bases hard each and every day. There are still plenty of individual players—Steve Finley, Craig Biggio, Bernie Williams, Ed Taubensee, Fernando Vina, Matt Williams, Jeff Bagwell, Luis Gonzalez—who run hard on every at-bat.

> **Inside Baseball**
>
> Take a stopwatch to a game and time the runners to first from when they make contact with the ball until they step on first. If the bases are 90 feet apart, right-handed hitters who run 4.4 seconds or better and left-handed hitters who run 4.2 seconds or better have major league speed. Interestingly, you will see many major leaguers loaf down the line, while others will run all out every time. As the scouts say, "The watch doesn't lie." I've often though how cool it would be to put the running times on the scoreboard like they do the radar gun readings.

Hustle to First Base

Moises Alou, Barry Bonds, Ken Griffey Jr., and many others just don't run hard to first unless they have a shot at a hit. I know; I time guys for a living, and I get 4.2 seconds on one at-bat (when a base hit can be had) and 5.5 on the next, then 4.2 on the next when another hit is a possibility (so that means they aren't hurting that day). I know that it is hard to play every day, but it doesn't take a great effort to run to first hard three or four times a night. I believe that this is one reason that so many players get leg injuries: they loaf for eight innings and then try to turn it on and beat out a hit in the ninth.

I cracked up when I read one day in the newspaper in Los Angeles that Gary Sheffield (who is a great runner) was upset with some of his teammates who weren't giving 100 percent; that night I timed him at 5.6 seconds to first base in his first at-bat in Dodger Stadium (when he hustles, he can do 4.2). In Las Vegas at a Triple-A game in 1989, I saw a so-called prospect pop up to the

middle of the diamond and just walk to the dugout with not so much as a step toward first base. I don't know what the manager did, but the player stayed in the game and played the next night. He was recalled to the big-league Padres later that year. What a bad message this is for players who do bust their butts every day.

Players can change.   In my opinion, Garret Anderson played like one of the laziest players in the majors in 1998, and none of the scouts that I talked to would have wanted him on their clubs. Then something happened. Some say Mo Vaughn talked to him (their lockers were next to each other when Vaughn arrived in Anaheim), but I'm really not sure what happened. The following year, Anderson became, according to my evaluation, one of the best hustlers in all of baseball. At-bat after at-bat he runs hard to first, plays much better defense, is the poster player for a great attitude, and is a fun player to watch. I never saw him loaf again, and I have recommended him for trades ever since. People who pay to see Garret Anderson play get their money's worth every game, and he is now, in my opinion, one of the top 10 players in all of baseball.

Running the Bases in Games

Your baserunning duties begin in the on-deck circle. You need to help any runners trying to score by telling them whether they need to slide or stand up. You can also help by getting the hitter's bat out of the way in case a player needs to slide.

The score and other game situations dictate everything that you do on the bases. When your team is behind by a lot, you must be conservative and the rest of the time very aggressive in your approach. When you get on base, you must ask yourself several questions.

Questions to Ask Yourself When You Get on Base

- What is the score, and what does my run represent?
- Is the third-base coach giving me a sign?
- Where is the defense playing?
- What kind of move does the pitcher have?
- What kind of arm does the catcher have, and does he like to throw?
- Does this team have any trick pickoff plays that I should be aware of?
- Should I tag up or go halfway if there is a deep fly ball?
- What kind of arms do the outfielders have?

Game Situations for Runners

When You Hit a Ground Ball

When you hit a ball on the ground to the left side, it is important that you don't watch the ball. It is natural to watch the ball on the right side of the field, but I do believe that it slows you down if you watch it on the left side. As you approach the bag, try not to jump, but instead use a forward body lean and step on the front edge of the bag with whichever foot comes up in stride. Remember to turn to the foul side after passing the bag, for you can get tagged out if you turn toward the second base side and the umpire thinks that you have made a turn in his judgment.

Inside Baseball

Watch closely when the count gets to 3–1 or 3–2 with either no outs or one out. Most teams have the runner or runners going on these counts automatically unless the manager stops them with a "don't go" sign. Of course runners automatically go with two outs and a 3-2 count.

When You Get a Base Hit

When you get a base hit to the outfield and a turn toward second is necessary, leave home plate with the idea that you are going for extra bases. While running toward first base, try to head directly for a spot about halfway between the base and the coach's box (about five feet right of the base). As you make the turn, step on the base on the inside edge closest to the pitcher's mound with whichever foot comes up in stride.

Make aggressive turns. If the ball is in left field, you should be able to get at least 20 feet past first base toward second before you hit the brakes and return to first. If the ball is in center field, you should still make a big turn, but you must be a little conservative on base hits to right field. As you reach the maximum in your turn and begin your retreat back to the bag, make sure you keep your eye on the ball as it is returned to the infield.

The mechanics of the turns are the same at all of the bases, except that you head directly at third and cut the angle a little sharper. Make sure you use your coaches as you are instructed. Remember that there are many plays that don't require the help of the coaches when the ball is in front of you. Develop a reputation as a player (and as a team) who makes aggressive turns, and before you know it opposing outfielders will be rushing plays and making mistakes.

Watch the ball. One of my pet peeves is the runner who gets a hit, makes a turn, and then turns his back on the ball as it is relayed back to the infield. You see many throws mishandled as they are relayed in, and this runner can't advance if there is a mishandled throw because he isn't watching the ball. It is also a good idea on a fly ball to hustle back to the bag, tag up, and take a few steps toward the next base, just in case something goes wrong with the relay.

When you are scoring a run and there is no play on you, it is important that you run hard all the way through the plate, especially with two outs. If one of the trail runners is tagged out before you cross the plate, your run doesn't count. I have seen three big-league games lost on this exact play just because someone was loafing.

Taking a Lead

When you are on first and you have asked yourself the important questions listed earlier, you are ready to assume your lead. Every player should have a plan that he uses to take his lead. Use this plan each and every time you take a lead, whether you are stealing, using the hit-and-run, or just getting your normal lead. Most players take a three- or four-step lead using the following technique. You should stay low, step out with your lead foot, and bring the rear foot up while keeping your feet spread at least shoulder-width apart at all times. Never take your eye off the pitcher, and stay with your plan. Using a bluff (a fake break) like Roberto Alomar often does disrupts the pitcher and the catcher. Some catchers will call a lot more fastballs when a good base stealer is on base.

Stealing a Base

Most players have to get a steal sign before they run. Some veterans and/or great base stealers will be given the green light—the right to steal whenever they get a good jump. Some big-league players like Jeff Bagwell, Craig Biggio, and others give each other signs when they are going to go. Players of this stature earn this right, and this privilege is not given out without great respect from the manager.

When the steal sign is on, getting enough of a jump to steal a base is just as much a mental skill as it is about speed. The unloading time (the elapsed time from the pitcher's first movement to when the ball gets to the catcher) and the pickoff move (or lack of one) of the pitcher are important factors in your overall success.

Much has been made of the unloading time during the past decade. The time from when the pitcher moves a muscle and unloads the ball to when the catcher receives it should be about 1.3 seconds or less. When you factor in the time that the catcher takes to receive the ball and throw it to second (1.8 seconds for Pudge Rodriguez and 2.2 for Mike Piazza), the overall time you have to steal the base is about 3.3 to 3.5 seconds. This doesn't sound like a lot of time, but remember that in addition, the throw needs to be accurate and the infielder has to tag you out.

The Mechanics of the Steal

The average for successful steals is just under 70 percent in the major leagues. When you are stealing, it's important to "stay down" on your break. So many runners stand up too soon and lose momentum. You should remain in the lower "driving" position (with forward body lean) at least until you are halfway to second.

Another important factor is the arm swing. If you use the "crossover" step (taking the left foot across the body to lead), then you should not throw your left arm across with it. Because you run naturally with your left foot in front and your right arm leading or your right foot in front and your left arm leading, having your left arm and left foot both in front on your first stride is unnatural. If you do it the wrong way as described, it may take you several strides to get in sync. To do it correctly, use the crossover step but fire out your right arm instead. This puts you in a natural running position and will feel so smooth if you have been breaking using the other method. The incorrect style was actually taught by some organizations years ago.

Many baserunners in the big leagues will look in and get the catcher's signs before they steal. If the runner can get a curve or a change-up to run on, it will increase his chances of success. Most catchers will use only one sign when there is not a runner on second, making it easy to pick up. It takes a lot of experience to look in for the sign and not get picked off in the process. Until you are a very polished player, you shouldn't try this advanced technique.

> **Inside Baseball**
>
> See if you can tell the difference between the regular delivery and a "slide step." Notice the location of the pitches when the pitcher uses this quick delivery. You will see that most pitchers normally throw a fastball when using a slide step.

Some people (television broadcasters) will tell you that you don't look in to see the ball contacted if you are stealing (as opposed to the hit-and-run). I believe that if you are stealing you look in on your second or third step as the ball gets to the hitting area. If you don't look, you can get doubled off on some balls, or you may be decoyed by an infielder into thinking the ball is on the ground, and you will be less aggressive going to third (because you don't know where the ball is). Baseball's cardinal rule on the bases is to always know where the ball is. It doesn't take any more time to look in and find the ball.

As you approach second base, forget the infielders. If you get into the habit of watching the fielders, they may fake fielding a grounder when the ball is actually popped up into the infield or outfield. If the ball is not hit, slide hard straight into the bag feetfirst. A headfirst slide is a stupid thing. You may break a finger, jam or dislocate a shoulder, or get all kinds of injuries sliding headfirst. I think that the only good thing about sliding headfirst is you get on ESPN. It is simply not worth it. The infielders will also be less aggressive tagging you and will be more likely to drop the ball or make another mistake when you go in feetfirst, hard, directly into the bag.

> **Inside Baseball**
>
> If you happen to have a great seat at a major league game, see if you can tell which runners will "peek" in to see the signs from their lead at first. Count how many times some of the best base stealers run when the pitcher throws off-speed pitches.

Recognizing Pickoff Moves

Right-handed pitchers must move (rotate) their front shoulders to throw home. Watch the left shoulder of the pitcher, and when it turns toward home, you break. Some base stealers use the front knee or the feet as keys, but I've always liked the front shoulder.

When you are stealing off a left-handed pitcher, remember that most give away their moves with their heads as they bring their right leg up. If they look toward home, they are coming to first, and if they look toward first (at you), they are probably going home. Some also give away their moves by the way they dip their back shoulder or their

> **Inside Baseball**
>
> Watch the baserunners bluff or fake a steal. This practice really upsets some pitchers, causing them to rush their deliveries. Roberto Alomar is one of the best at this.

back leg. If their shoulders stay level, they are going to the plate and you can break, but if their back shoulder gets lower than their front, they are probably coming to first. You and your coaches must study the lefties to discover one of these giveaways. Because most lefties make up their mind whether to throw over or not when they come set, some players get a shorter lead and go on the first move the left-handed pitcher makes. Whether you are a fast runner or not, this works very well in high school and college.

Other Game Situations

Hit-and-Run

The major league average success rate for the hit-and-run is only 36 percent. A manager should know his personnel well when using this play.

When you are the runner on a hit-and-run, you are not looking for a "stealing jump." You will make sure the pitcher is going to the plate before you break. Although you still have the same lead, mentally you are not looking for a great jump, so it should be impossible for you to get picked off.

You look in on your second or third step and see the ball as it gets into the hitting area. Then you just react to the ball. Obviously, you will keep going if it

Inside Baseball

Sit on the first-base side sometime when a left-handed pitcher is pitching. See if you can tell when he's coming over to first on a pickoff attempt.

is on the ground. If the ball is hit on the ground at somebody in the infield, you will slide into the base. If there is a line drive at an infielder, you also keep going because there is just no way to get back. If there is a fly ball, you break stride and stop, reading the ball and reacting to it. Because you know where the defense is playing, there will be balls hit that will not require you to break stride to look at the fielders in order to advance. For instance, say you are on first and the ball is hit over your head down the right-field line. You have already noticed that the rightfielder is playing toward right-center and will therefore have no chance to catch the ball. On this play, you will not look back but keep going, round second, and pick up your third-base coach after you round the bag.

The Secondary Lead

When you are on first or any other base, you must develop a "secondary lead" when the pitch is on its way to the plate. Most good baserunners use a "shuffle step" or simply hop two or three times, keeping their shoulders parallel to the baseline after the pitcher goes home. You should do this on every single pitch when you are on the bases.

It's important that you time this move so that your right foot is hitting the ground just as the ball gets to the hitting area. Remember to keep your shoulders parallel to the line and square with the plate. If the ball is hit, you can then cross over left over right and go. If the ball is taken by the hitter or swung through, you will plant your right foot, cross over right over left, and return to the base quickly. The secondary lead is an important part of being a good baserunner. I think that Roberto Alomar and Bernie Williams get the best secondary leads that I have seen.

Sacrifice Bunt

If you are on first and a bunt sign is given, assume your normal lead, and let the play develop. You must get to your secondary lead and wait until you see the ball on the ground before you cross over and go. Be careful if the hitter bunts through (misses) the ball, for lots of teams have an automatic pickoff attempt after a missed bunt.

Men on first and second, sacrifice bunt in order.   Listen to your third-base coach and his warning about the short-stop and second baseman. Keep your eye on the pitcher. Get a good secondary lead.

Inside Baseball

Watch each runner and see if he is consistent with his secondary leads. He should do it correctly regardless of how many pitches the pitcher makes while he is on base. Many players start out doing it well, but as more and more pitches are made, they get less and less aggressive in their leads.

Man on second.   If you are on second, never forget that you are in scoring position. This means that everything you do, your entire approach, is built around scoring a run. Make sure that you know where the defense is playing.

When assuming your primary lead, make sure that you know where the short-stop and second baseman are playing, and then watch the pitcher and listen to your third-base coach. You are better off with what I call a "safe maximum lead" than to get too far out where you are jockeying back and forth to the base. If you are a smart runner, then this approach eliminates the need for the third-base coach to protect you with voice commands. This safe maximum lead is about 10 to 12 feet (three or four steps). At this distance, even if an infielder were standing on second base, he wouldn't be able to pick you off. This might not sound like it is enough, but remember that the ability to score is based on your secondary lead,

Inside Baseball

Some infielders use the voice commands of the third-base coach to pick off the runner. For example, the shortstop comes in behind the runner, and as he returns to his position and the coach says something like, "You're OK," the runner may take an extra step, and the second baseman breaks and the pickoff is on.

not on your primary lead. This will give you the best chance at a great jump as well as the ability to get back on a pickoff from the catcher. When you are on second base with two outs and there are two strikes on the hitter, you should break when the hitter swings.

If you are going to attempt to steal third, you must be 100 percent sure. Nothing is worse than having a runner thrown out who is already in scoring position. In my opinion, the only time you should attempt a steal of third is with one out. With no outs, you are probably going to score anyway, and with two outs it is just a dumb play.

When on second, be careful of the "inside move." This is a move by the pitcher that simulates his delivery to the plate. The right-handed pitcher lifts his left leg and spins clockwise and fakes or throws to second.

When you are on second with no outs, you must tag up on a long fly ball. If you return to second and tag and the ball falls, you should be able to score anyway. If the ball is caught and you can tag and reach third with one out, you have considerably increased your chances to score.

When you tag up, never leave early, for someone on the field will see you. Remember to tag up on all foul balls with fewer than two outs.

Too much is made of the so-called rules like "Make the ball be through in front of you." There are many balls that you can advance on in front of you if you are aware of a few simple keys. If the third baseman must come in too far to make the play on the ball, you can advance easily. If the shortstop is playing up the middle holding you close and the ball is hit sharply in the hole toward third, why should you not advance? The shortstop can't get that ball with a normal effort, and not only can you get a good jump, you can score easily. If you hesitate before breaking toward third, the chances are the third-base coach will have to hold you up. If the ball is topped weakly down the third-base line, you may also advance easily even if it violates the silly rule here. Good baserunners are aggressive.

Man on third, infield playing back. If you are on third base and the infield is playing back, it means that the defense is willing to trade an out for a run. You should be aggressive, but remember that there are some ground balls that you can't score on even when the infield is back. If the ball is hit sharply to third or back to the pitcher, you may get trapped if you break too soon. Because this defensive positioning indicates that the defense has a considerable lead in the game, you need to be careful and make sure that the ball is hit to the shortstop, second baseman, or first baseman before breaking for the plate.

Be sure that you freeze on line drives and tag on all balls hit to the outfield medium depth or longer. It is also important to tag up on all foul balls and watch out for a wild pitch or passed ball.

Man on third, infield playing in. In this situation, make sure the ball is on the ground and is through the infield before you break for the plate. Ask the third-base coach what he wants you to do if he doesn't give you instructions. Watch for the wild pitch or a passed ball. Follow the same rules as already given regarding line drives, fly balls, and foul balls.

> **Inside Baseball**
>
> Watch the runner on third and see if he gives away a squeeze by his body language. Many runners look to the hitter, to the pitcher, and back to the hitter in an unnatural way when the squeeze is on. Watch for the hitter to tap the bat on his shoe, run his hand up the bat, or go into the box with his front foot first. These are all common answers to the squeeze sign, which confirms that he has the sign from the coach.

Potential squeeze. On the squeeze, the third-base coach will let you know with a word sign, a touch sign (touching a certain part of your body with his hand), or a conventional sign. At any rate, this is no time to goon out or to not pay attention. Not only can you cost your team an important run, but you can get badly hurt with a missed sign (if you break and the hitter swings away). For this reason, most teams have an answer (a confirmation sign) to the squeeze from the hitter.

When the pitcher starts forward with his arm, or when his front foot hits (this is roughly the same instant), you break for the plate. Be a good actor and don't give it away early by acting like something great is about to happen; be cool.

If you are going to be out by a mile, stop and get into a run-down. They may throw the ball away, or at least any trail runners can move up before you are tagged out.

Some managers use a "safety squeeze," which requires the runner on third to wait until he sees the ball on the ground before he breaks for home.

Additional Baserunning Tips

When you are on base, you should form a mental picture of the defensive coverage. Just as if you are on a blimp over the field, you can see where everyone is playing in your mind. If you use this skill, many times when the ball is hit, you can break without having to turn and look at the defense first.

When breaking up a double play, slide toward the shortstop side of second base when the second baseman is turning the double play, because he will most likely go across the bag. When the shortstop is the middleman on the play, slide to the first-base side to disrupt him as he comes across to make the throw.

If you get a hit and the winning run is trying to score from second with fewer than two outs, make your turn and keep going to second (the defense can't cut it off). If the runner is thrown out at the plate, you will be in scoring position instead of on first.

Inside Baseball

Watch how the coaches are constantly reminding the baserunners of the situation. During an at-bat, a good coach will remind the runner of the outs and other information over and over again after each pitch.

Profiles on Great Baserunners

Not Fast, Just Smart (Jeff Bagwell)

I picked Jeff because I think that he is the smartest baserunner in the big leagues. He doesn't have blazing speed, but he steals bases with a great success ratio (nearly 200 for a power guy is unbelievable). He always goes from first to third on routine base hits and scores well over 100 runs every year. I have watched him as a coach (1991–1993) and as a scout (1994–present) in hundreds of big-league games, and I've never seen him make a mistake—never. Nobody makes turns any better; he cuts the corners with perfect mechanics and execution. He hits the inside corner of the bag (nearest the mound) every time with whichever foot comes up in stride.

Know Your Opponents (Tony Gwynn)

Although he wasn't fast in his last few years, Tony Gwynn is underappreciated as a baserunner. He could almost steal at will in his younger days, but even when he became slower, he could still go from first to third and score runs on base hits that others couldn't. The guy paid attention and knew his opponents as well as anyone. I don't recall ever seeing him get doubled off with a line drive or hesitate when the ball was hit to the area of the field where nobody was positioned. This indicates that he always knew where the defense was playing.

Just Pure Speed (Rickey Henderson)

Henderson will go down in history because of his stolen bases, but his greatest accomplishment is his runs scored. Hand in hand with that is his ability to get on base over his career. As far as stealing, I watched him in Oakland, and I believe that this is one part of the game that he really prepared for. Some will say that he just had God-given speed, but I think he must have spent considerable time watching pitchers' moves and having a plan.

Put Out Every At-Bat (Steve Finley)

He always knows the game situation, what his run represents, and which outfielders and catchers can throw him out and which he can take liberties with. Finley not only hustles like teammates Matt Williams and Luis Gonzalez, but he is a smart player on both sides of the ball. He has great balance and control of his body. Through his winter workouts, he has maintained his speed throughout the years. Although most players lose considerable speed in their mid- to late-thirties, he can still run a 4.0 to first base when he needs to. He is also one player who knows when to use his coaches and when to be on his own as far as going from first to third.

People pay good money to watch professional baseball, and when you come to watch players like Steve Finley, you never get cheated—they give you full effort.

Baseball Relationships

Players and Their Coaches

As a player, you may develop a special bond with a coach. This relationship can last a lifetime and border on magic. Some players and coaches communicate so well that each seems to know what the other is thinking during competition. You may have had many teachers in school who have had a terrific impact on your life. You may remember some of your teachers for a long time, but when you've been lucky enough to have a good coach, the positive impact lasts a lifetime.

Your coach has an opportunity to teach you things that your parents can't or don't take the time to teach you. He or she can be a terrific role model for you, or, if a coach is misguided, he or she can come close to destroying you as a human being. Whatever the case, coaches make a difference, good or bad, during your baseball playing days and for the rest of your life.

Listen to your coaches, whether you are a big leaguer or in Little League. Ask questions of them, accept their criticism as well as their praise, and learn from your mistakes. The knowledge and experience they pass on to you can become valuable tools to help you become the best that you can be and reach your goals.

Just Win, Baby

When coaching, you should teach players how to win and how to lose. Winning is better than losing, but learning how to accept both in a gracious way while keeping the game in perspective is essential.

> "Winning is important to me, but what brings me real joy is the experience of being fully engaged in whatever I'm doing."
>
> —Phil Jackson, Los Angeles Lakers coach

I think an important message that every coach should pass on to players is that if they work hard and learn the fundamentals of baseball, the wins will follow. This holds true for eight-year-olds and major leaguers alike. When coaches emphasize positive things, they create an atmosphere that produces positive results. Players who become accustomed to succeeding will succeed. Players who prepare in practice and work hard expect to win. Winning might not be the only goal, but it becomes a habit, especially if you prepare in practice and get your club ready and expecting to win each game.

Players and Parents

In college and pro baseball, we rarely deal with parents, at least directly. They show up, some are a little pushy, but basically they just stay out of the way. Their sons are nearly men, and they let them run their own careers.

At the San Diego School of Baseball, I have met some of the greatest parents in the world—people who give up things for themselves in order to send their children to us for private lessons in hitting, pitching, and fielding.

You can tell when the players on a team like each other and are having fun. The manager and coaches must create an atmosphere that promotes fun. In youth league baseball there is usually the same close-knit feeling among the parents. In my travels, I have also seen jealousy among the adults and have witnessed several ugly scenes over the years in all parts of the country. See the section on "Case Studies—Players and Coaches in Action" in Chapter 2.

Mistakes Parents Make

Most parents make mistakes while having the best intentions. Parents who get too high emotionally when their kid wins are sending the wrong message. If your enthusiasm is missing after a loss, the player can get depressed feeling that he or she has let you down. It is important that parents stay on an even keel and try not making a big deal of the wins or losses. Instead, focus on the effort and attitude, then try and move on to the rest of the day. Change the subject after a good game or a bad game.

A friend of mine, Dr. Fran Pirozzolo, a famous sports psychologist, says that sports can be life-defining. I believe that sports can make or break a young person's will and ability to succeed in life. I know that this sounds awfully heavy, but I have seen the good and the bad in youth sports.

Controlling parents produce kids who are full of self-doubt and are afraid to make their own decisions. One of the worst practices is offering a bribe for winning. The message is clear to the kids that winning is the only important thing—it must be or you wouldn't be offering a gift for the win. Bribes for home runs are just as potentially damaging for the player emotionally as they are mechanically. A player who is offered a gift for individual performance may forget the team concept and have a tendency to try to do too much, with failure the predictable outcome.

In youth league baseball, parents, especially the dads, get out of line much too often. Although most parents know their place and are supportive, you always have a few whose sole purpose seems to be second-guessing. They usually don't want to help, but they seem to always have the answers. In extreme cases, violent or at least unacceptable behavior is an all-too-common occurrence.

The hitters can't hear you.   The heart rate of a hitter soars up to 140 beats a minute while in the batter's box. Most young hitters cannot process much information effectively at this stress level, and additional instructions simply don't help at this moment. In fact, hitting tips from parents between pitches probably do more harm than good. The same is true for pitchers and players playing defense. If they are listening to you, they can't be concentrating on the game. Although random instructions shouted from the side can come from many sources, parents commonly shout buzzwords like *concentrate* or *focus*. Most of the time, these words mean nothing to the players and just put more pressure on them. In fact, most young guys I talk to think that words like *concentrate* shouted during a game mean to try harder.

It is true that some players have overbearing dads. We have all seen dads in youth baseball or high school ball stand on the sidelines and shout instructions for everyone to hear even though his son or daughter has a coach sitting a few feet away in the dugout. I wish I could explain to these parents how much damage they are really doing to the player, as players only become confused when they receive mixed messages.

Violence in Youth Sports

Several unsettling incidents have taken place in the past few years. A baseball coach in Florida attacked an umpire and broke his jaw after a game, and a hockey dad in the Northeast beat another dad to death in the parking lot. In a soccer game in South Brunswick, New Jersey, a dozen parents ended the game with a fistfight while 20 or so eight- and nine-year-olds watched. These horror stories happen more and more often.

Dads Coaching Sons

Some of the real problems in youth baseball come from dads who are coaches to their sons. They expect too much and put way too much pressure on their own sons to be some kind of "perfect" players. Some dads who coach their sons seem to be embarrassed when their sons make a simple mistake, a mistake that every other player makes when learning the game of baseball.

We asked 300 kids if they had played for their dads and, if so, did they like it, and why or why not.

42 percent said they have played or are playing for their fathers.

Of those, 62 percent said they would have preferred *not* to play for their fathers. The most common reasons why they didn't like it were that the pressure to perform was too great and they felt awkward or funny in front of the other kids.

The second most common reason why they didn't like it was that their dads expected too much from them.

75 percent told us that they felt that they disappointed their fathers on a regular basis.

65 percent felt that their fathers were too hard on them when they coached them.

An Extreme Case

I knew one major league player whose father called him in the clubhouse after games. Sometimes 15 minutes after a bad game the phone would ring and his dad would point out all of the bad things that he had done (as if he needed to hear that he struck out three times). I saw him in tears by his locker more than once, for he felt that he could never please his dad. This was a 25-year-old player making more than a million dollars a year. His father was still pulling the same stuff years later after his son had become an All-Star in the majors.

Players and Other Players

Learn to Love Your Teammates

The single greatest thing about playing baseball is the relationships that you develop with teammates. The kidding, the friendships, and the feelings of team-work and working together are the greatest things about team sports. Most people will be on teams the rest of their lives in the business world. The trust and the feelings of accomplishing things together as a unit make you feel almost like your family makes you feel. This is the thing I miss most about playing. These relationships last a lifetime; enjoy them, for you will remember them forever.

Competing and Having Fun for Life

I recently played in a 55-and-over softball league with old friends whom I hadn't seen much in the past 20 years. We never missed a beat. The jokes, laughing at the bad plays, and everything was the same as it had been when some of us were trying to make a go of a baseball career 35 years earlier. Even the winning and losing meant something, at least a little something. I played with a player named Tom Whelan in college and against him in pro baseball (he was with the Cubs organization). He is the most intense competitor I have ever known. Now 30 years later, playing slow-pitch softball, he is as competitive as ever. He plays fair, displays good sportsmanship, and doesn't make excuses, but he just hates to lose. There is nothing wrong with this approach to the game.

The bodies don't look the same, the power is gone, the speed is a joke, but the fun and the competition, the camaraderie and the friendships remain the same. The camaraderie and fun are what most players miss when their careers are over.

Set an Example

Older players should be reminded that they are role models and mentors for younger kids. Young kids want to be like their big brothers and sisters. This can be a burden for older players or older brothers and sisters. Although most of the time kids are not even aware of this burden, it is very real. Because there are very few true leaders in the world, and because that means that most players are followers, it is important that the older players and adults set a proper example.

Camaraderie and Team Chemistry

The Oakland A's of 1996 had something special. Manager Art Howe always creates a friendly atmosphere on the teams he manages, but this was a unique situation for me. Players Mark McGwire, Mike Bordick, Terry Steinbach, Billy Taylor, Jason Giambi, Scott Brosius, and others were the ultimate team players.

Inside Baseball

Watch the dugout after runners score. If the players have the "team thing" going, they will all get to their feet and congratulate the player who just scored without being reminded each time. Selfish players just don't have the time.

We had great coaches and fun players, and behind all the clubhouse pranks and fun was all-world equipment guru Steve Vuchinich. When you have fun on a team it means more productivity and overachievement. With a $13 million payroll and all rookies in the starting rotation, we still competed. The next year, Bordick, Brosius, McGwire, and Steinbach were all gone, and we signed Jose Canseco, who in my opinion was the complete opposite of a team guy. We were headed in the right direction and, bang, the fun and the attitude were gone. It took three years for Art Howe to rebuild the attitude and finally win in 2000.

Having veteran players around makes a team click. The young guys need experienced guys like these to talk to. I believe that Jason Giambi's career took off and he developed into an MVP-type player in part because of Mark McGwire. The coaches also need guys like these to bounce ideas off of. The manager needs veteran players to provide leadership on the club. As a pitching coach, I can't tell you how much I appreciated All-Star catcher Terry Steinbach (calling the game), Mike Bordick (setting the defense), and Mark McGwire (setting an example for all). I had a little sign with Mark, and he would go in to the pitcher and either chew him out or pump him up. Mark didn't need a lot of guidance from me, for he seemed to always know what to say to the pitchers. Sometimes the people in the front office think that the game is played on their laptops with numbers and statistics. It is not. Baseball is a game played by human beings, and emotions play a huge part. Computers can't tell you what is inside of a player.

Respecting Your Teammates

Respecting the feelings of your teammates is important. When you are having a great day with four hits, enjoy it, but keep any wild displays of emotion in check. Somewhere in the clubhouse or dugout there may be someone who has struck out three times, and he may not want to hear it. If you are lucky, he will show you the same respect when it's your turn to have a bad day.

Players and Bullies

Kids can be very cruel. Although we don't put up with any insensitive behavior at the San Diego School of Baseball, it happens, even around us. Kids are so sensitive, and adults should be attentive to the needs of children who are at risk. Kids who are overweight, who have a poor complexion, or who have speech impediments might make easy targets for a bully lying in wait. Sometimes small kids or poor players can also be targets.

Tips for Future Pros
Good players never show up the opposing team by yelling negative things from the dugout or behaving unprofessionally.

Coaches and parents must look closely to spot these kinds of potential bullying situations. Remember that bullies are basically cowards and are very good at picking on other players when adults are not around. It is the responsibility of every adult to protect at-risk players and others from the assault of these bullies. Protection begins with each and every adult setting a good example with his or her own behavior. If your child sees you making fun of people, he or she will see it not only as acceptable but possibly as funny or cute.

I'm all in favor of making kids take responsibility and do their work, but out-bursts of temper, shouting, and/or physical abuse are not acceptable or necessary to teach and motivate players. Parents should monitor games and practices for coaches who bully and demean players in the name of discipline and building toughness. This behavior can damage kids for a lifetime, and coaches who display this kind of behavior should not be coaching.

Fifteen percent of the kids we talked to report having been hit, slapped, or kicked by a coach in the past two years.

Players and Agents

Agents came into the game of baseball in the past 25 years. Former superagent Jerry Kapstein was the first I ever met, and for the most part I like the ones that I know. I think most have their clients' best interests at heart and do a fine job representing them. I don't think that players need agents until they get to the big leagues, but almost everyone has one as soon as he gets drafted by a pro team or unofficially (as an adviser) even before the draft. As I said, most are honest, but there are plenty of crooks out there.

Just because an agent is certified (the Major League Baseball Players Association has a list), that doesn't mean that he or she is capable. Whenever an agent approaches you, ask for a client list, and ask if he or she minds if you call a client or two. If the agent objects to this, find someone else. Good agents can help you make money. What they can't do, and shouldn't try to do, is accelerate or advance your career. Make sure your agent stays away from the field per-sonnel and watches your career from a distance. More than once I have seen aggressive agents hurt players with a pushy attitude. A good agent will tell you the truth on where you stand in the industry. There will always be others (who are trying to steal you away) who will tell you what you want to hear. Don't lie to yourself about how good you really are.

Millions for Everyone

Based on what's happened to salaries in the past 10 years, the agents must be doing something right. The present system (which the owners have created with poor judgment) favors the players so much that it has driven the game into a critical state. The players haven't done anything wrong. The owners are 100 percent responsible for the mess that the business of baseball is in. Big-time agents like Scott Boras, John Boggs, Barry Axelrod, Tommy Tanzer, Tony Antanasio, and others have just been better at their jobs than the owners have been at theirs.

Players and the Media

As a player you have a responsibility to have a professional relationship with the media. You can be friendly, but only to a point. You should have mutual trust and respect, but don't forget that some reporters are never off duty. It will take you years to figure out which ones you can trust. Some writers who cover a club can become buddies, and you can have a lot of laughs with them, while with others there is no such thing as "off the record." Try to be honest, but never let down your guard.

Tips for Future Pros

A class player treats everyone from the clubhouse kids and the fans to the owner in the same professional way.

"How Dare You Pick on ME?"

Media members get in trouble with the players because of mixed messages. A star player who is used to being fussed over all his life takes it personally when a writer tells everyone that he is not doing the job. He reacts in an angry way because nobody else in his life may have ever questioned his ability and/or desire. If others around him (like coaches and agents) had been honest with him from the beginning, perhaps he could handle the criticism in a better way.

"I Won't Talk Anymore"

I really think it's terrible when players refuse to talk to the media or hide in the training rooms after games so they don't have to comment on their poor performances. When these same guys have great games, they are usually standing in front of their lockers waiting for the press when the game is over. A responsible player is consistent with his treatment of the media as a whole. Remember that the media can either help or hurt your career, and reporters are people with feelings just like you.

Hey, We're in Show Business

We need characters in baseball. As much as I root against him, Barry Bonds is a unique guy; he's entertaining, and he's good for baseball. John Kruk was a personality and was good for baseball. Guys like John Rocker (even though he says stupid things) and Jose Canseco (self-consumed but a drawing card) put people in the seats to love them or hate them. Active and former players Mark "the Bird" Fidrych, Mickey Hatcher, Sammy Sosa, Jose Lima, Turk Wendell, Jason Giambi, David Wells, and other guys with colorful personalities add something to the enjoyment of the game for fans. Let your emotions go, and have fun playing baseball.

We are in the entertainment business, and the media is an important part of the overall success of our game. As a coach, you may choose to use the media to send a positive message. For example, after a pitcher has three bad starts in a row, you may tell a sportswriter that you are "with the pitcher all the way." It's nice when a coach tells a player to his face that he supports him, but it is very special when he and his teammates read it in the paper. But be sure you mean what you say. You will look very foolish if you pull him from the rotation after one more start.

Negative comments should always be made to the player one-on-one and not in the media. Coaches who try to motivate with public comments of a negative nature won't be happy with the results.

> **Inside Baseball**
>
> As the managers and umpires come out to exchange lineup cards on the first night of the series, the home manager (or a coach that he sends up there) will go over the ground rules of the ballpark. After the first night, the conversation turns to jokes, talk about the weather, and just general baseball talk.

Umpires and Everyone Else

Volunteer Umpires

Coaches should set a good example for their players with umpire relations. The umpires at the youth level are volunteers, and even the best are going to make mistakes. Coaches should encourage their players to treat umpires with respect, and parents and other spectators should adhere to a strict code of conduct. I suggest using the term "Mr. Umpire" instead of calling the umpires "Blue." This is a good start toward positive umpire relations.

Coaches should never use umpires as an excuse for a loss, for that just opens the "excuse door" for the players, who will quickly follow. Before you know it, you have a bunch of excuse-making kids with an easy out for their failures.

Professional Umpires

In professional baseball, arguing with umpires becomes part of the game, part of the entertainment package. Nine times out of ten, players, coaches, and managers are never that mad, and at least part of their arguing is just for show. Most umpires that I know are very professional men who care deeply for their jobs and for the integrity of the game. Sadly, a few umpires have taken on an arrogant attitude in the past few years. I remember one veteran umpire who always had a chip on his shoulder. I went to the mound in Atlanta to talk with my pitcher one day, and he met me there. He said in a gruff voice, "Let's go," and I said, "Can I have a minute to talk to my pitcher?" and he said, "You've already had enough time to tell him everything that you know." He obviously wanted to throw somebody out of the game that day. I was smart enough not to take the bait.

Most people don't realize that almost all of these umpires work for up to 10 years in the minors with lousy pay to get their chance at the big time, and most are very appreciative of the opportunity.

Players must respect or at least pretend to respect and like umpires, who are normally trying their best. You must respect the effort. I have refereed some basketball, and I'll tell you that being an official is a very tough job.

Inside Baseball

When a player strikes out on what he thinks is a questionable pitch, watch him as he leaves the plate mumbling. A good umpire will look straight ahead pretending to ignore him. An umpire with an attitude will take a step or two toward the player inviting him to escalate the potential argument. Watch the umpire's partners in the field; they will sometimes keep an eye on the player as he reaches the dugout so they can report later if he threw a helmet or bat or turned and shouted one last comment.

Different strike zones for star players.   It is true that some star players have different strike zones. It is true that some great pitchers get more of the plate than others get. Some umpires will tell you that star players have earned that. Another thing I've noticed is that catchers get the benefit of a doubt, I guess because the plate umpire has to face the catcher each inning behind the plate. I say a ball should be a ball and a strike should be a strike, no matter who's hitting or pitching.

> **Tips for Future Pros**
>
> The more you squawk, the more things will go against you, so, as they say, "Shut up and play." Take my advice: say hello, be pleasant, and give the umpires the benefit of the doubt. You've got your hands full just being a player.

Players and the Fans

Players have a responsibility to communicate with the fans. Sadly, this is the part of marketing that baseball has ignored. Teams open the gates when the home team is almost finished hitting and ready to go inside the clubhouse. Because most clubs don't take infield practice very often, the next time the fans see the players is right before the game when they are getting ready. Most players will sign autographs if you catch them at the right time. The problem is that baseball has never allowed the fans any access at the "right" time. The truth is, most kids never get an autograph or even get close to their idols. Thousands of kids send their baseball cards and other memorabilia to the club for the players to sign, and if the player is a star, it may be months before the cards are returned signed. In some cases, the cards are lost, autographs are forged, or cards are simply left in a box somewhere and the kids never see them again.

How to Become a Major League Player

Life in the Major Leagues

I was lucky enough to coach in both the American League and the National League for a number of years. Outside of the travel, which is a killer, the life is second to none. You travel first-class on chartered aircraft, stay in the best hotels, get paid well, receive the finest insurance for life, and get more than $70 meal money each day. The major league pension is the best by far of any in the world. In addition to having access to great investment programs supplied by the Major League Baseball Players Association, a player, coach, or trainer with 10 years on the pension can retire at up to $80,000 a year beginning at age 45, or well over $115,000 a year if he waits until age 60 or so. I would recommend the professional baseball life to any young player. The difficult part is getting there.

Talk Is Cheap

Players tell me they want to become big leaguers, and then their coaches tell me they don't show up for practices. Lots of players talk a good game, but their actions just don't support their claims. Parents say, "He lives, sleeps, and eats baseball," and I watch him and he is not motivated to work on his skills. He likes to hit, he likes to have a uniform on, he likes to play the game of baseball, but the average kid doesn't want to work at getting better. Each generation that I have watched for the past 30 years has had a worse work ethic than the one before. Who is at fault here? It is too easy to blame the parents. Is it the kids themselves? I don't know; I don't think anyone has the answer. I still see some great players with real fires inside, young men who will be a success at something in their lives. I still see some parents who push just hard enough—being supportive but not obsessed—but more and more, there are parents and kids who have their priorities way out of line.

A Very Diffucult Game

Baseball is a very difficult game to play. The fundamentals of baseball require thousands of hours to master. I laugh when a parent calls me and says, "My son has been an All-Star for three years now, he plays on a travel (or select) team (a team that recruits the best players), and he really doesn't need any more fundamentals." I find out that the kid is 11 or 12. Everyone needs more work on fundamentals. Baseball is a game of endless repetition and practice, yet some kids say, "Well, I know that basic stuff, so now I want to learn advanced baseball." Sure there are things in this book that baseball people will call advanced, but the truth is you never stop learning and improving your basics.

Why is it that when every new major league manager is hired, the first thing he says is, "We are going back to basics and work on the fundamentals"? Poor baseball fundamentals or the lack of execution of the basics will result in more lost games than anything else will. Even in the big leagues, games are lost every night because of poor baserunning and/or defensive mistakes. From youth baseball to the majors, defensive and baserunning lapses happen in every game. Too many players and coaches just don't think that fundamentals are that important.

Tips for Future Pros

Professional players manage their emotions. Displays of temper don't show a competitive attitude, just a lack of emotional control.

I have known many kids who couldn't make it in baseball but have gone on to excel in other sports. We had a player in our baseball school in the 1980s named Brock Glover who was just an average baseball player, but he became a world-class motocross champion and made millions of dollars. John Lynch was a very good player in our school (drafted by the Florida Marlins), but he chose to play in the National Football League instead and became a star. Almost everyone knows a story of a kid who couldn't make it in baseball but turned out to be a great high school or college soccer star. I have seen many kids who can't hit a baseball but go on to become terrific golfers. Baseball is truly the most difficult sport in the world to play at a very high level.

Some players make their mark in other sports and then turn to baseball. Old friends Tony Gwynn and Graig Nettles were known for their basketball skills until age 20. I played high school baseball with Nettles, and, to be honest, we had five or six better players on our high school team in 1962, and none of the others went very far in baseball.

Maturity Level Is a Big Factor

Maturity levels come in to play with baseball as in no other sport. Some players are still little kids at age 12, and other 12-year-olds need a shave in fifth period. In Little League I played against two particular players who were the same age but very mature and much stronger, faster, and more talented than I and every other player in the league. Neither one of these young men went on to play even in high school.

In American Legion baseball, I remember facing a pitcher named Dave Morehead, an 18-year-old man who had a heavy beard as a senior in high school. I was a 15-year-old sophomore with no body hair and peach fuzz on my face. Although I was a good hitter for my age, I was never so overmatched in my life. Dave Morehead went on to pitch in the majors for the Boston Red Sox and some other clubs. At age 14, I faced another kid named Dale Twombly in Pony League; he was a man who threw very hard, and I was a scared little kid. He hit my friend Bruce Nelson in the ribs. When the air was forced out of Bruce's lungs, he made a high-pitched sound that I will never forget. I was up next. I was frozen and never swung from my position in the back of the box. That fear went away gradually, but I remember the emotions I felt to this day, and that was more than 40 years ago.

Tips for Future Pros

Baseball is a game that consumes you. If you are not committed to the game, don't choose it as a career. If you are not willing to work at it nearly every day all year long, don't waste your time.

An Emotional Game

Baseball is a game of emotion, passion, and respect. Watching an eight-year-old get his or her first base hit, reach first base, and look for his or her parents in the stands still gets to me. Watching a major league rookie get his first hit or first win does the same thing to me. I have seen hundreds of each of these situations happen, and they still affect me the way they did the first time. If seeing the look on a player's face when he makes a great play or gets a game-winning hit doesn't affect you emotionally, you shouldn't be coaching. I cried like a baby when Darryl Kile threw his no-hitter when I was his pitching coach. I cried when Alan Trammell was named Most Valuable Player of the 1984 World Series even though I was working for the Padres, who were his opponents in the series that year. I got emotional again when "Tram" got his 1,000th RBI, even though it was against my pitchers in Oakland. I knew what kind of special person he is. Alan is a good guy who worked so hard and remained a good person through all of his success. I cried when Dave Smith (whom I signed to his first contract and later coached in Houston) was honored in the Astrodome for his 216 lifetime saves. I was upset for a week (I think I still am) when the A's traded Mark McGwire. I watched him stand in the clubhouse July 31, 1997, and hug all of the coaches and players and cry his eyes out. He had grown up an Oakland Athletic and was being traded away. I will always remember that I was on the same team with a living legend and, more important, a very good human being.

I still get warm inside when I watch a father as he explains the game to his son at a major league or minor league game. Hey, I'm sorry, but that is the way baseball affects a person like me who has lived the game every day since he was six years old. I try to never forget that baseball is about the kids.

Putting the Game in Perspective

To succeed at this game as a player, as a coach, or in any position, you must have a passion for it and at the same time realize that it is just a game. On Opening Day in 1991, I was standing in the bullpen in Cincinnati next to Cy Young Award–winner Mike Scott, who was our Opening Day pitcher. It was during the Gulf War, and our troops were in the middle of it in Iraq. Before the game, the sellout crowd stood and applauded a tribute to the men and women of the armed forces, and the song "God Bless the USA" by Lee Greenwood was playing as the Blue Angels buzzed the field. I was holding back the tears thinking about how lucky I was to be an American, in uniform, doing what I loved. I lost it. Suddenly the game didn't mean much compared to human beings shooting at each other on the other side of the world.

A similar scene was repeated in September 2001, when major league baseball returned after the terrorist attacks. I think people from all over the country put sports into its proper perspective and now think about what is really important in their lives.

What Do Scouts Look For?

Be honest with yourself. If you are a position player and can't run fast and don't have any power, you're probably not going to play in the major leagues. If you are a pitcher and can't throw a fastball 75 miles an hour at age 18, you may never generate any interest from scouts. When you get out of college and your fastball is more than 85 miles per hour, you might get a shot. Scouts are looking for players with the tools to play professionally and players who will someday develop into major leaguers. If you can run to first base in 4.4 seconds from the right side or 4.2 seconds from the left side or faster, you have big-league speed, and scouts will be interested in you providing that you can do some other things well (like hit).

Tips for Future Pros

If you want to be noticed by a scout, hustle. We scouts are human, and attitudes count. If you can't play well and have no skills, it won't matter, but if you are on the fence ability-wise, it might make the difference.

A scout must be able to project your skills to be at a higher level by the time you are 22 or 23 years old. If you are a very physically mature individual at age 18, a scout may feel that you may not improve your physical tools all that much in the next few years. Scouts should be looking instead for "young 18-year-olds" who may have baby faces and long skinny limbs, but who have lots of room for growth. More and more every year, scouts are looking to the colleges for sources of talent.

Tips for Future Pros

There are very few college scholarships available for the number of players who want them. If you "walk on" to a college program, expect a less-than-fair opportunity. Consider a community college if you are not a four-year school prospect.

Go to College

If you can't do the things that I've described as attractive to scouts and you are not drafted in the June draft, go to school. Baseball is fun, but a college education will last a lifetime. College baseball is a wonderful experience, and you shouldn't miss it. By giving yourself time to mature and develop, you could make yourself into a prospect.

Four examples of late bloomers are Eric Karros, Darryl Kile, Art Howe, and Mark McGwire. Eric was not even close to a prospect out of high school (I was his hitting coach, and I know). He walked on at UCLA and later became a big-league star for the Dodgers. The Astros drafted Darryl Kile very late in the draft and hoped that the gangly, uncoordinated, skinny kid who threw 80 would improve. Scouts Reggie Waller and Ross Sapp believed he would, and they signed him. He now throws 92 to 93 mph and is an All-Star. Art Howe attended a tryout camp for the Pirates when he was 24 years old after being passed up in the June draft. He has played and managed for more than 20 years in the majors. Skinny Mark McGwire so impressed the Montreal Expos with his power as a senior in high school that they drafted him as a *pitcher*. He didn't sign, went to USC, and grew up to be a slugger. Hall of Famer Tom Seaver was five feet, nine inches, and 160 pounds out of high school. He grew up in college and went on to win more than 300 games and was one of the hardest throwers in baseball.

If you are worried about being seen by scouts, don't be. Scouts from all big-league teams cover every college in America.

Never Give Up

Lots of players sign late in the draft or sign after not being drafted at all. Some players spend many years in the minors, are released more than once, and still get to the majors after a long and frustrating career riding the buses. Recently retired pitcher Billy Taylor (Padres, Cardinals, A's, Devil Rays, and others) pitched for 14 years in the minors before getting his chance. He later became the closer for Oakland, saved more than 100 games, and made more than two million dollars after the age of 34. It is never too late for players with marginal ability and big hearts.

Tryout Camps

Major League Baseball holds tryout camps all over the country beginning in June every year. For a list of tryout dates and locations, check mlb.com. Individual scouts also have tryouts at high schools and colleges from time to time. An interested player should ask his coach about them.

Even though major league players like Art Howe and MVP Kevin Mitchell were signed out of tryout camps, few players make the major leagues this way. Your best shot at being discovered will be by playing on a team and showing scouts the aforementioned skills during games. Most high school teams and every college team in the country are scouted by all professional teams.

The Baseball Draft and the Money

In the year he was signed by the Dodgers, more than 1,200 players were drafted ahead of Mike Piazza. There were more than 50 players taken ahead of Tony Gwynn the year the Padres drafted the superstar, and almost the same number was drafted ahead of 20-year shortstop and six-time All-Star Alan Trammell of the Detroit Tigers. The Padres passed on Dwight Gooden and took journeyman pitcher Jimmy Jones and then took Ray Hayward instead of Roger Clemens the following year. This doesn't mean that the Padres had bad scouts—in fact, their scouts were terrific—it's just a very hard job.

In 1985, the White Sox drafted a catcher named Curt Brown instead of taking Barry Bonds, and in 1995 the Oakland A's took pitcher Ariel Prieto and passed on Todd Helton. I believe that scouting is the most difficult job in professional baseball. Every organization in baseball has stories like these—bad drafts and bad trades that they try to forget with time. One thing that all organizations have in common: they scout the West heavily. In the first 25 years of the draft, 25 percent of all players drafted were from California.

If you are looking to baseball to make a lot of money, you are looking at the right sport, but please stay realistic about your chances. Only a very few players ever make big money in baseball. About 1,000 players in the world make a good living in baseball. Several thousand more ride buses all night, are paid $850 per month or less, and never get close to the bigs. Only 5 percent of the players who sign contracts ever play one day in the majors.

The salaries have escalated out of control for nearly two decades. The sad state that baseball is in now is the fault of the owners, period. They have never trusted each other, and the large-market teams as well as the middle-market teams have acted irresponsibly for as long as I can remember. Anybody who blames the players is just not paying attention. Most players I know are embarrassed to make the money they make, but the attitude is, "They are giving it away, so why not take it?" Players like Mark McGwire and Tony Gwynn have taken much less than the fair market value to stay put and be happy. McGwire wanted to be loyal to his teammates, his manager Tony LaRussa, and his personal trainer Barry Weinberg. This act showed the real character of the man. There are lots of players who feel like this. To put yourself in their place, you must ask yourself, if the boss of a competing company offered to double your salary, would you accept it? This is exactly what has happened to the players over the past 20 years.

Travel or Select Baseball

The original concept of travel ball was that by playing against better competition, players would improve more rapidly. Most experts will tell you that there simply is no evidence that this is true. There is evidence that players who play too much baseball will get burned out and quit.

Basically, travel ball is an effort to separate the best players from the ones who aren't as good so that the skilled players can face better competition. The parents pay up to eight thousand dollars a year for each player to play on these special teams. I talk to lots of kids who prefer to stay in their neighborhoods and play with their buddies. Ten-year-olds don't need to travel all weekend (some teams travel two weekends a month or more) to play against strangers. What they do need is to have some playing time around home and maybe spend more time with their family members and friends.

These select teams are happening in both baseball and softball. High school coaches will tell you that most of their varsity players have played travel ball. Sure, most of the varsity kids played travel ball; now there are so many travel or select teams in California that any kid with enough money and average ability can get a spot. What about the kids who can't afford to "pay for play"? How about the kids who do play for travel teams but don't play much? The people who run these teams can keep the best players only if they win, and there are no rules to provide for innings played by team members. Nobody ever improves while sitting on the bench.

On these teams, coaches are paid by parents, and although some of the teams have parents who know how to act, some parents are just plain obnoxious. Some parents want their sons and daughters to lead off and pitch or to play shortstop and hit cleanup. These types of parents drive the good coaches away. There is also a war going on between teams—raiding players and bad-mouthing the rival coaches. Young players hear and see all of this and learn all kinds of horrible behavior. This type of parental pushiness has even shown up in high school and college ball, with aggressive parents trying to force quality coaches out. I know at least 20 great high school coaches who have quit over the years because of the way parents act. It seems that the more affluent the area is, the more problems coaches have with parents.

> **We asked more than five hundred kids what they thought of "travel" or "select" teams.**
>
> 62 percent said that they have played on or have been asked to play on these teams.
>
> Of those that had experience on these teams, 55 percent said that they played because their parents thought it was a good idea, and only 22 percent said that they really enjoyed the experience, with some describing the experience as being just "OK."
>
> 75 percent said that they wish they didn't have to travel so much to play games.
>
> Only 33 percent said that they got better coaching by playing on these teams.

My Kid's an All-Star

In my opinion, Little League makes a big mistake naming All-Star teams. It can be devastating to the kids who don't make it. Labeling kids at any age is a dangerous practice. Did you know that 90 percent of the kids playing Little League are told sometime in June, "Your season is over; we'll see you next year"? The truth is that lots of kids lose interest after being told, "You're not good enough." Do you know how many kids don't even show great skills until age 12 or 13? What about those late bloomers? I have seen many kids in our school who are simply awful at age 10 and terrific at age 13. They just need a chance to play. Why don't we just play a longer season? Why do we have to cut loose 90 percent of the kids (more than two million) with two months to go in the summer? So we can have playoffs and a Little League World Series for a few hundred kids?

The whole thing is now out of control. With 31 million boys and girls playing sports in America, we now focus on a couple hundred kids playing in Williamsport in August. I counted 27 games televised during the Little League World Series, and I read that 600,000 households were watching. Why can't all that energy be pumped into extending the season for the rest of the players?

Baseball "Showcases" and Schools

Several "showcases" claim to offer exposure to college and pro scouts. While some operations are on the up-and-up, many are stealing money from high school players and their parents. These companies say they will videotape you and send the tape to the college coaches of your choice. Most college coaches pay no attention to these tapes and accompanying recommendations.

Tips for Future Pros

I have met many players who make an All-Star team or an All-League team and then stop working on their fundamentals. This is a huge mistake. There is always someone else out there willing to keep working, and they will pass you by.

Although we have had many players make it to the professional ranks in the past 30 years, we fully recognize that our students attend the San Diego School of Baseball and All Star Softball to improve their skills. We have never made any promises, implied or otherwise, that our goal is to get players signed to contracts.

There is a terrific lure to professional sports for young athletes. One operation in Florida that grosses more than $20 million a year cashes in on this lure. There are lots of these companies throughout the world. They offer scholarships to many players around the world to attend baseball, tennis, golf, and other schools. They fully recognize that only about 3 percent of the players attending will become professionals. The other 97 percent or so pay the freight. These operations have been called "seductive traps" and "dream factories." I personally don't see anything wrong with parents sacrificing a little to help their sons and daughters chase a dream, even when the odds are against them. I spent $100,000 to send my daughters to film school, so what's the difference? I've never regretted it. Both of my daughters are successful in the industry, my wife and I sacrificed a lot to help them, and we feel good about that.

Baseball Is Hard Enough

Baseball is a game that has plenty of negative things built in. In soccer you can hide in the middle of the field when you're not very good. Nobody strikes out with the bases loaded to end the game in most sports. Even the best players make lots of outs in baseball and softball. I know parents who keep moving their kids up further and further, level after level, until they can't compete anymore, lose confidence, and quit. Why can't people see that there is nothing wrong with being a big fish in a little pond, allowing a young player to gain confidence and a sense of self-worth that can last a lifetime?

The Awful "B" Word—Burnout

When does encouragement stop and pushing begin? Nobody is immune to poor judgment. My daughter Amber was nine and attended a recreational gymnastics program one day a week for two hours. When she started to display great ability and win meets, we moved her to two nights a week, then three, then at age 10, four nights a week, four hours a night. She was still winning when she took me for a walk on the beach and told me she would like to take some time off.

I told her that she could do whatever she wanted to do. I was disappointed because I liked the experience of going to the meets and seeing her get her 9.8s and 9.9s while winning award after award. I even had visions of her competing in high school or whatever. But my daughter was burned out at age 10. Although I am considered an expert in the area of kids and sports, the "burnout" concept escaped me completely when it came to my own daughter. Amber never returned to the gym. She turned out to be very successful, as both my daughters have, but I'll always wonder if she could have been a champion without me pushing and increasing her workouts to the breaking point.

Things Parents and Coaches Can Do to Help Avoid Sports Burnout and Other Big Problems in Their Kids

- Promote their interest in things other than sports.
- Don't let them play any sport year-round.
- Encourage your kids to play lots of different sports.
- If you coach your own kids, don't hit them third and pitch them Opening Day. Hit them seventh, and bring them in relief in the first game. Make them earn an important place in the order. Make sure they take their turns playing right field and sitting on the bench.
- Be supportive of the coaches and the umpires, at least in front of your son or daughter.
- Don't make excuses for your kids (bad calls, bad luck, and so on). They need to take responsibility for their own actions.
- Be consistent in your attitude after the game, good game or bad.
- When you go to the batting range to practice, keep your kids in a cage that is easy for them, and remember that 50 to 100 swings are plenty. More is not always better.

Thousands of Great People and a Few Jerks

I love Little League and other youth programs. I have hundreds of friends involved in these fine programs. I have met a few bad people. I love the volunteers who are usually wonderful parents and others who do so much for the kids. I just wish they used more sense when it comes to playing time, letting players play different positions, and so on. As we have discussed, kids are so smart, and they listen to everything adults say, and coaches have a terrific impact on their players.

Respect for the Game of Baseball

I feel proud to have stayed in pro baseball for 35 years. I have a great respect for major league players and the game itself. It is really hard to make it to the big leagues and stay there. I think that my attitude about all this pretty much represents how the majority of professional players, coaches, scouts, and front office people feel.

I know so many wonderful baseball players like Luis Gonzalez, Steve Finley, Alan Trammell, and others who are genuinely nice to everyone they come in contact with. I'll never know what makes other players stiff a kid for an autograph or not run hard to first base every time.

When I was a coach in the big leagues, I tried to sign all of the autographs I could when none of the players were available. I was standing in the dugout in Fenway Park when batting practice was over one day, just looking around that historic ballpark. All of the players somehow missed a cute little guy standing there with his glove held out to be signed. As I walked over to him on my way into the clubhouse, he held out the glove for me to sign, I signed, and he said, "Excuse me, sir, is anyone *good* coming out to sign?" Sometimes coaches fall into the category of "better than nothing" when it comes to autographs.

We asked several hundred kids, "How does it make you feel when a sports star gets in trouble with the law?"

65 percent said it made them feel "sad" or "disgusted."

The most popular comment was, "How can they blow it when they had it made? They must be very stupid."

Another popular comment (44 percent) was, "I think that they should be thrown out of baseball."

Not one single kid said, "They should be forgiven and given another chance" or "Everyone makes mistakes"; not one responded that way.

Pick the Right Role Models

How can players like Darryl Strawberry and Steve Howe be given chance after chance after getting in serious legal trouble and embarrassing themselves and the game of baseball, which they say they love? How can players be reinstated so quickly after hitting their wives? How about the kids who have baseball cards of those players on their walls at home? Who speaks for those kids? Major League Baseball doesn't seem to care enough about how little kids who love baseball and worship big-league stars might feel about this behavior.

In the early 1980s, Joan Kroc, who was the owner of the San Diego Padres, in connection with her Operation Cork, founded the present-day treatment programs in the minors. Prior to that movement, players with alcohol or drug problems were just released and forgotten about. To this day, there is still a sub-standard education program in place throughout professional baseball.

One Chance, Then Banned for Life

My take on all of it has always been that everyone makes mistakes and should be given one chance if they use drugs. After that, a lifetime ban should be enforced. Of course, the major leagues don't even have drug testing for big-league players, only for minor league players. When a player breaks the law, second chances turn into third and fourth chances. Isn't it funny that players keep getting chances as long as they are good players who can help somebody win and make money for the owners?

Athletes Are Slipping with the Kids

It makes me sad to hear that according to experts the percentage of kids who think that athletes are "cool" has dropped more than 50 percent in recent years. Athletes are also no longer tops on the lists of the people that kids would most like to meet or that they consider a good role model.

Good parents have quit trying to promote athletes, movie stars, and others as role models to their kids and have become role models themselves.

Index